D0228320

Inspirational Manager

JUDITH LEARY-JOYCE

Inspirational Manager

How to build relationships that deliver results

PEARSON
Prentice Hall
BUSINESS

Harlow, England • London • New York • Boston • San Francisco • Toronto • Sydney • Tokyo • Singapore • Hong Kong
Seoul • Taipei • New Delhi • Cape Town • Madrid • Mexico City • Amsterdam • Munich • Paris • Milan

PEARSON EDUCATION LIMITED

Edinburgh Gate
Harlow CM20 2JE
Tel: +44 (0)1279 623623
Fax: +44 (0)1279 431059
Website: www.pearsoned.co.uk

First published in Great Britain in 2007

ISBN: 978-0-273-71251-0

British Library Cataloguing-in-Publication Data
A catalogue record for this book is available from the British Library

10 9 8 7 6 5 4 3
11 10 09 08

Typeset in 9.5pt Iowan by 3
Printed and bound in Great Britain by Ashford Colour Press Ltd., Gosport

The Publisher's policy is to use paper manufactured from sustainable forests.

This book is dedicated to all managers

You too can be inspirational.
I'm rooting for you!

*Our greatest fear is not that we are inadequate,
but that we are powerful beyond measure.*

Marianne Williamson

Contents

About the author

Judith Leary-Joyce has a real passion for developing great workplaces and wants everyone to get out of bed each morning, eager to get on with their work. As CEO of Great Companies Consulting, she spends her time supporting organisations that have an appetite for delivering great results through their people. She has considerable experience of consulting plus coaching/facilitating leaders, managers and significant influencers in a wide range of organisations. Her psychology background gives her a deep understanding of the factors that drive people to make their best efforts and perform brilliantly.

Judith is also author of *Becoming an Employer of Choice* a book that explores how you can contribute to the development and maintenance of a great workplace.

Foreword

If you have ever been lucky enough to have experienced working with an inspirational manager you will know the tremendous value they create for you personally and also for the organisation. We have probably all had the reverse experience of working with a manager who isn't that great, and we know the negative impact that they can have. By the fact that you are reading this book, I suspect that you are on a personal quest to be an inspirational manager yourself. You might already be there but just not know it, or you might have already discovered the tough challenges that you encounter in being a manager.

This book sets out in a practical and pragmatic way the route towards becoming that inspirational manager. The key insights throughout the book are based on research and real life case studies. This isn't all about theory, it has been generated by studying some of the very best managers – who better to learn from?

Every organisation is striving to enhance performance and to differentiate themselves to become an employer of choice. If you believe in the philosophy of Employee Engagement, then you will know inspirational managers are an essential ingredient in creating an engaged organisation.

The value of organisational leadership is well known, but the value of everyday inspirational management seems less well understood. It is true that every leader has to manage and every manager has to lead. This book focuses on the essentials of great management and how this can make a difference to the lives of many people and to the success of the organisation.

The key lessons set out by Judith Leary-Joyce should be understood by all of us who have the responsibility of being a manager. *Inspirational Manager* should ideally be used as a well 'thumbed' reference guide as well as an inspirational read in its own right. As each chapter unfolds, you will discover new and exciting insights.

Good luck with your quest!

Matthew Brearley – UK HR Director
Vodafone UK Limited

Acknowledgements

No one writes a book alone – at least not the way I've chosen to do it. It's actually quite a sociable affair!

When I had the idea for this book, I spoke to my PA, Sue Simmons, who did her best not to wince! I contacted some companies that I knew had won Employer of Choice awards and asked if I could speak to their best manager. As I discovered when I wrote my last book, they were remarkably welcoming and open, so very soon we were on our way.

The first task was to get some meeting dates booked and, fortunately, once Sue focuses her mind, there is no stopping her! Manoeuvring my complex jigsaw of a diary, she arranged appointments for me to meet the managers and organised all my other work around it. When I hit those moments of overwhelm, it was Sue who kept me going. You are reading this today because I couldn't bear for all her determination to go to waste.

The research stage was the best bit. I spent six months travelling around the country talking to some stunning people, their teams and their own managers. It was really exciting and I always left the discussions feeling invigorated, inspired and quite sure that writing this book was the right thing to do.

I did have one solitary section in the middle of the process when my husband stuck a label marked 'Quiet, author at work' on the conservatory door. If you ever think of writing a book, don't do it when the builders are around! My one contact in that very intense month was Stephen Partridge, editor of my last book, who knows me and my style well. As ever, he helped me stay on track, suggested great ideas for the format and kept me laughing with wonderful stories of his family and experiences. He has been a sage and a mentor throughout.

Sixty-five thousands words and a sore arm later, I met Samantha Jackson, my editor at Prentice Hall, and the sociable side returned. Sam has been a real steadying influence, encouraging me always to write in a way that will make the content most valuable for you, the inspirational manager.

Of course I needed a reader – someone who would tell me the brutal truth when I needed to hear it. John Leary-Joyce – husband, CEO and Executive Coach – was that man! He sat in bed late at night and early morning reading, scribbling and pondering. The toughest conversation came when he realised the third rewrite of a chapter was still not right. He girded his loins and told me the truth – like every inspirational manager must. He also sat patiently while I stormed about the place, then made me tea as I started all over again. I hope you'll agree, he was right to 'expect the best'.

Once the book was ready, Sue then began the complex process of making sure everyone agreed with what I'd written about them. The office was like a war room with heads spinning, endless cups of tea and occasional heart-warming chats on the phone to 'our managers'. We feel now as if we know them really well.

My team of GCC consultants were constantly there in the background, reminding me of my passion for great companies and inspirational managers – people *must* be treated with respect and enjoy the many hours they spend at work, life is just too short for anything else. They read, advised and challenged my thinking and we have had great fun together, exploring how to convey this material in an 'inspirational' style for our clients.

Of course, I can't finish without saying a huge 'THANK YOU' to all the inspirational managers, the managers of the inspirational managers and their fantastic teams who spoke so openly about their work, their mistakes and successes. It has been a huge honour to work with you all and I have many memories I shall treasure.

Judith Leary-Joyce

As part of the research for this book, Judith interviewed HR Directors from the organisations involved to find out how they support the development of Inspirational Managers. In order to read the important insights from this original research visit **www.greatcompaniesconsulting.com** and enter the password IMHR0607.

CHAPTER 1

It's got to be better than this!

'I'd love this job if it wasn't for the people.' You can be forgiven for feeling like that sometimes, because management is hard work. The workload is a struggle, the boss is demanding, customers just make for problems and, on top of it all, you have to manage the people. It is a huge task!

But there must be more to it, otherwise why would some people love it so much? Take Helena Moore, at Bromford Housing Group, for example. Her greatest satisfaction is in seeing people develop. She accepts that there are low moments in the job, but they are far outweighed by the highs. And Paul Dunmore from Thomson Directories: he likes to help people when they are struggling. He has had his own hard times and people were there to help him, so he is delighted to return the favour.

In fact, inspirational managers are as important as great leaders. There are no Employer of Choice awards without brilliant management capability. Without you building great teams, your workplace will never be one of the best. You are that significant!

❝ Inspirational managers are as important
as great leaders. ❞

The benefits of being an inspirational manager

So, from the organisation's point of view, you need to be performing at the top of your game, but is there any personal benefit from doing so? In fact, improving your management capability will bring big benefits for you, your team and the organisation.

▶ You will become known as a fantastic person to work for and high-flyers will flock to your door.

▶ You will get a reputation for being straightforward and trustworthy – traits that others admire and value.

▶ You will have good relationships across the management community, so there will be plenty of peers willing to support and help you.

- The greater sense of meaning and purpose in your life will be highly satisfying.
- Young people will name you as their role model – what a compliment!
- Your results will be significantly better than they are now, increasing your bonus and chances of promotion.

All of this means that you can go home satisfied at the end of the day, have a relaxed time with your family and friends and sleep easy in your bed. How does that sound?

The *Field of Dreams*

It sounds extremely good to me and is exactly why I wrote this book. Did you ever see that movie *Field of Dreams*? Kevin Costner builds a baseball pitch in his cornfield especially for the best players of all time. He does it because he hears a voice saying 'If you build it, they will come'.

This book is my cornfield. It's not academic – it is more like a handbook full of stories of real live managers and practical actions you can take. I wrote it because I would love *you* to be an inspirational manager, then you, your people and your workplace will all reap the benefits.

❝ I would love you to be an inspirational manager. ❞

Twelve inspirational managers have helped me by speaking openly about what they do well and where they go wrong. None of them is perfect – no one is – but hearing how they work with their people was a brilliant experience for me and one that I want to pass on to you.

The people you will meet are:

- Charlotte Butterfield, Badenoch & Clark
- Paul Dunmore, Thomson Directories
- Della Garmory, Nationwide
- Oliver Hickson, Central Office of Information (COI)
- Tesh Kataria, Tower Homes (London and Quadrant Housing Group)

- Nic Larkin, Data Connection
- Ian Martin, Diamond Trading Company (DTC)
- Helena Moore, Bromford Housing Group
- Allison Nicoll, Freedom Finance
- Fran Rodgers, Northampton Borough Council
- Andrew Rothesay, Boehringer Ingelheim
- Ben Wood, Mace.

I know that they are inspirational because I also spoke to their teams and their own managers. I really hope the members of your team speak about you in such glowing terms – if not right now, then in the near future – because it was so energising. They didn't just paint pictures of perfection – they included both the fantastic and the shortfalls – but the striking thing throughout was the commitment they had to their managers and each other. They were all totally focused on the success of their teams.

You will also hear from some of their own managers, who were equally generous with their time and energy. Providing support to people who are constantly striving, learning and demanding of themselves is an interesting job and one that keeps these managers on their toes.

Now over to you

So now I'm handing the baton over to you. I'm not saying it will happen all at once – even Kevin Costner had to wait. Being an inspirational manager takes determination, willingness to get it wrong and commitment to yourself and your people, but you will get there if you really want to.

It depends how wedded you are to life as it stands or if you would prefer more excitement, challenge and fun. Of course that wonderful sense of having done something worthwhile and productive to take home with you at the end of the day. It's your call.

Being an inspirational manager is remarkably simple in theory – it is just about building strong relationships and being trustworthy. We all know how to do that, don't we? Maybe not. Maybe we are not prepared to put in the time and effort required. On the other hand, this is exactly what inspirational managers do and so, I hope, will you as you progress through this book.

CHAPTER

2

What it takes to be an inspirational manager

'Be approachable. If you're not approachable, you are not managing.'

Danielle Holyoak, Freedom Finance

'It's a partnership,' says Paul Dunmore, at Thomson Directories. 'I work with each one of my direct reports to ensure the best outcome for them personally, for the team and the company. Without this, they might just as well work on their own.' This level of support and challenge is the difference between being an inspirational manager and just pinning the title on your door. It is also the difference between exceptional and mediocre performance.

We have all heard tales of really terrible managers and most of us will have worked for OK and even good managers. Unfortunately, far fewer can claim to have reported to a truly inspirational manager. These are the ones who help people achieve their full potential by telling it the way it is – even when the going gets tough – and giving loads of encouragement and support. Direct reports still talk of them fondly, even after 20 years. They are the ones who get the job done, develop their own potential *and* enjoy their life at work.

Wouldn't you like people to talk about how inspirational you are? This book is all about *you* being that memorable, getting the best from your people and delivering extraordinary results for your organisation. It is a really exciting proposition and one that means you can walk out at the end of the day feeling proud of what you and your people have achieved.

So you want to be an inspirational manager

The first step on the journey is to understand where you are now, because being an inspirational manager is no easy job. It requires:

▶ a willingness to put others before yourself

▶ an iron will, as you hold them to the task

▶ the humility to admit when you are wrong

- the flexibility to change when necessary
- a sense of order and orderliness.

Stories of great managers are inspiring and exciting, but that is only half of it. We mustn't forget the filling in appraisal forms and time management required to deliver fine team results, while also achieving your personal objectives, plus all the efforts involved in keeping the headcount at the right level.

Liking people is not enough on its own. You also have to be organised and willing to follow the processes and procedures laid down by your organisation. Getting the best from a large number of people and delivering exceptional business results requires systems.

- You have to be fair to everyone, which means following tried and tested pathways set down by the organisation.
- If you are a rebel or hate paperwork, you will have to find a way to overcome your scruples so you can fulfil management expectations.
- Legislation dictates that information must be kept and behaviour monitored.
- You have to fulfil your HR obligations regarding appraisal and measurement.

You don't have to like it, but you must be prepared to do it and do it well. It is true of all areas of life. We all love the exciting, fun and interesting bits, like football and the theatre, but you still have to do the washing-up and shopping. If you don't, life becomes very uncomfortable and eventually grinds to a halt. It is just the same in management. Don't think you can get away without form-filling and procedures – they keep the wheels turning and work suffers if you let them slide.

However, this book isn't about that side of management. There are plenty of other books out there that will help you and probably an HR function that can provide you with the relevant information. This book is about that supposedly 'soft' side of management – caring for and developing people. The hardest stuff you will ever be asked to do!

&& 'Soft' side of management ... The hardest stuff you will ... do! &&

How do you manage now?

Let's begin by taking a quick look at your present style. What follows are questions from a 360-degree questionnaire based on the behaviour of inspirational managers in organisations that have received Employer of Choice awards, so it provides a real opportunity to measure yourself against positive role models.

If you want to get the best out of this exercise, I'd encourage you to think only of what you actually do, not your good intentions. But it is hard because most of us fall short of those ideals some or even most of the time. It is so much easier to massage the truth, to only look in mirrors when the lighting is kind. Unfortunately, there is no easy way to becoming an inspirational manager. The saying that you 'get out what you put in' holds true for this self-assessment. This sort of honesty takes courage, but then inspirational managers are courageous people.

And there is one more step to consider that shows a real willingness to change. Give the questions to your direct reports and see what they say. Only then will you really know what you are like as a manager, because these are the people who experience the truth on a day-to-day basis. Asking them will show you exactly where to focus your attention. If you really want to get the most from the exercise be honest with your choice of people – don't just go for those people you know will be kind. It will be a lot more helpful to know what people *really* think.

A word of warning

If you do decide to ask others, let them know that you really want to hear the truth and that you will accept what they say. Their feedback may not immediately ring true or fit how you understand yourself. It can even seem shockingly unfair. However, it is their experience, regardless of your intention. This is the tough thing about 360-degree feedback. You need to understand that perceptions vary and the same world can look very different to other people. This is where we hit the philosophical bit – you will never find just one truth, just many different perceptions of reality, so, whatever you intend, you have to deal with how *other* people experience you.

However you decide to use this exercise, no one else will know, unless you choose to tell them, so you have everything to go for and nothing to lose except your illusions!

Inspirational manager 360-degree feedback questionnaire

Answer each question twice:

- first, how effective you are at this behaviour
- second, how important this behaviour is in your present job.

Use the following scale.

	1	2	3	4
For effectiveness:	Never	Occasionally	Usually	Always
For importance:	Not important at all	Occasionally important	Important	Critically important

Statement	For effectiveness				For importance			
	1	2	3	4	1	2	3	4
Takes time to get to know people beyond the superficial								
Is visible and approachable in the workplace								
Addresses inappropriate behaviour with clear unambiguous feedback								
Recognises and respects the importance of 'life outside work' to self and others								
Encourages others to learn from their mistakes								
Listens first in order to understand another's perspective								
Makes others feel valued as individuals								

Source: © Great Companies Consulting Ltd

Results

The ideal is for both sides to match up. If you think your job only occasionally requires you to listen first in order to understand, then mark the importance of that as a two. If you believe that you only occasionally do this, then the effectiveness is also a two, which shows that you are on the right track according to your understanding. There is nothing worse than a manager spending time on something that is not really important for the job. So, if your numbers match up, then you can be pleased with yourself.

However, the reality is that if you rate any of these questions as less than four for importance, you are not yet thinking like an inspirational manager. All the areas mentioned are essential in the inspirational manager toolbox and, when done properly, will add considerably to your personal satisfaction.

Depending on your results, read the following section and see which description matches you best.

What sort of manager are you?

People come into management with different sorts of skills, some of which work better than others.

The tactical manager

Maybe you are a tactical manager:

▶ You enjoy delivering on processes and procedures because you recognise how important they are to the smooth running of the organisation and it is what you enjoy.

▶ You have appraisals done on time and all the paperwork that goes with it.

▶ You put a lot of effort into recruitment, so that you have the best people in your team.

▶ You ensure that everyone has the latest information from the top team.

All this is essential to the management role so don't stop! It will deliver results and you will be the darling of the organisers, but there is more to do if you want to be an inspirational manager. Tactics alone will never build a devoted team.

Tactical managers have really organised minds, are totally reliable and people recognise how efficient they are, but still it is not always great to work for them. It is the lack of heart that does it. Sure, appraisals are done according to the book, but there is no time to chat, discuss some exciting ideas or get a bit of wholehearted praise for once. That would be too much of a distraction from the 'day job'.

Equally organised people will love working for a tactical manager, but for big picture thinkers or risk takers, you will be a nightmare. The trick is to find a job that will benefit from being kept under control and avoid a team that needs to go outside the box, because that would be unbearable for you unless very clear limits are set. But that, of course, would reduce the usefulness of the risk takers to the business and the end result will be miserable people all round. It is back to that lovely mantra of great companies – right person, right job.

66 *Right person, right job.* 99

You will know you are a tactical manager if you love that feeling of doing the right things at the right time. The trick is to understand why you do it.

- ▶ Is it because the processes help you manage your people?
- ▶ Do you take delight in delivering organised and clear outputs for their own sake?

A bit like being house-proud, you need to be clear whether your delight is in having the pristine house for the sake of it or in making life easier and more comfortable for the inhabitants.

Action

▶ If you just love the tactical stuff of management, make an assessment of how much time you spend on processes and how much on people. If the balance is weighted firmly on the process side, consider buddying up with another manager who enjoys the people side but is less good with processes and see how you can support each other.

▶ If you like processes because they help people to do their jobs well, you can start redressing the balance straight away by putting time in your diary to take each of them out for a coffee and an informal chat. Use the time to get to know them a bit better, in and out of work. The output you want from this time is an enjoyable conversation – which will help build your relationship and make it easier to do appraisals at the end of the year.

▶ In addition, build yourself a support system. Find a mentor or bring together a small group of aspiring managers in your company. Have lunch together once a month and talk about how you are all getting on. Share what has worked well and pick their brains when something didn't work well.

The split manager

This situation arises when organisations use management as a development tool. It is a good idea when used well, but can lead to problems in terms of workload. The split manager has one or two direct reports from a related area, in addition to doing his or her own job. Because the reports do different work, there is no chance of delegation, so the pressure increases.

The classic split manager is:

▶ successful in their job, so has a heavy workload and a lot of responsibility

▶ managing one or two people, because the boss wants them to get some management experience.

▶ unable to delegate because their reports are not directly linked to their area of work.

Finding time for people management in this situation is really tough.

15

Sometimes the split manager ends up not knowing which way to turn and the apparent promotion feels like a poisoned chalice.

If this fits your situation, you need to look at every option for freeing up some time or manage the time you have to within an inch of your life! If in doubt, talk it through with your own manager, making clear what is and is not possible – not least to manage their expectations.

❝ *People ignored take up far more time than people well tended.* **❞**

The big thing to remember is that giving too little time to the management bit of your work will only add to your burden. People ignored take up far more time than people well tended. So, it will be time well spent to get to know your people and set clear objectives and goals. It is a paradox, but giving time up front will enable you to get on with your own work. Ignore them until they blow and your own schedule will be shot to pieces.

Action

▶ Find a quiet room and map out all the areas of your job – specific tasks, personal development challenges, management of people. Look at the outputs required and the objectives you have for the year. Now look at the cycle of the year. When will you be most busy with your own work? When are appraisals due and how long do you have to complete them? Add in any other particular demands of your job.

▶ Once you have mapped it all out, make a plan for your time. How much do you need to spend in each zone? Include some regular time with your direct reports in order to stay on top of their needs. This means that they will be less likely to disrupt the plan and it will reduce the number of shocks.

▶ Once you have made your decision, book time in your diary straight away for the one-to-ones with your direct reports, to make sure they don't slip under pressure. Make sure that you get your own one-to-one time with your boss, too, because you need the support.

The effective manager

Then we come to the effective manager, split and not split. The bulk of managers fall into this category and, if you include yourself here, good on you! Managing people is not an easy job and if you do it well, then you are serving the team and the organisation. Being an effective manager, you realise the importance of the tactical stuff, so produce things on time and in the right order. You prepare for appraisals and discuss them with your people, you give them objectives to work to and track how they are getting on over the year and you produce good results for the company.

As an effective manager you:

- have clear team guidelines in place
- ensure that everyone has clear and measurable objectives and give the help they need to achieve them
- complete an effective appraisal and return it to HR in good time
- make sure that each person has a development plan they can work to
- understand how to recruit the right people to your team and follow procedures well
- deal with underperformance as soon as it presents a problem
- keep on top of your own work and deliver on your personal objectives.

If you are doing all these things, your team will be working well and the organisation will be happy with what you deliver. My guess is that you are one of two things:

- satisfied at the end of the day that you have done your best
- happy enough, but suspect that there is something more to this job of managing people.

If you are in the second camp, you are ready to be an inspirational manager!

Moving from effective to inspirational

The real difference between effective and inspirational is the intention that lies behind what you do. Effective managers do the right thing because they know it makes sense and it is what the job needs. Inspirational managers go the extra mile because:

- they want to see their people shine
- they care about their team members for their own sake and want them to achieve the best they can

- they have strong beliefs that drive them to do things really well
- they understand the truth about 'tough' love – that it is a sign of real respect
- they want to enjoy their work.

❝ The real difference between effective and inspirational is the intention that lies behind what you do. ❞

In essence, they bring their emotions to the job as well as their minds and they build exceptional relationships – this is what makes the difference.

Action

Think about the people you work with and consider how well you know them. Include your emotional response as data and try out your intuition on the following questions.

- Will they come to you with problems as soon as they arise?
- Do you understand what drives them and what they are passionate about?
- Do you know the people above you well enough to advocate for the team when you need to?

None of these things are vital in the usual sense and you can still deliver good results without them, but it will stop you delivering *exceptional* results. It will also stop you from having a team who say 'we are proud of our manager and work really hard to make them a success'.

❝ We are proud of our manager. ❞

The value of emotions

'It's all very well to say I need to apply my emotions to be a great manager, but what on earth does that mean?'

In fact it requires you to rethink management. If any of the following statements feel true, you may be more inspirational than you realise. If they feel unfamiliar, ponder them now.

- Team values are something we all agree on and are proud to follow.
- Appraisal time is something to be anticipated and treasured. ➤

It is my prime motivational tool, so I make sure that I am well prepared.

▶ Recruiting the right person is one of the most important things I do.

▶ Telling the hard truth is the greatest gift to an underperformer – if I don't care enough to be honest, who will?

▶ At least 50 per cent of my time is spent on managing people. I know it is worth it because I can see my protégés in a number of top jobs and I feel really proud of that.

If you agree wholeheartedly, my guess is that you run a strong team in a way that is fun and exciting. Your people know who the boss is, despite being so fond of you. You collaborate with them whenever possible, make decisions when you need to and work is a really positive place to be. Another spin-off is that other managers respect you and ask your advice. They have noticed that fantastic people choose to work for you because it is career-enhancing and they would like to be chosen in the same way.

Paragon of virtue? Too good to be true? I know it sounds a bit much, but I have met some of these managers and there is a lot you can learn from their good behaviour and their mistakes. They have been really honest out of a desire to help you move forward. It is all part of the same process: they enjoy the idea of helping other people move forward, even when they may never see you!

Action

▶ Find your advocates and supporters in the organisation and discuss ways in which you can support each other.

▶ Use this book as a starting point and work your way through the chapters and action plans.

▶ Challenge your thinking, particularly in areas where the answers seem totally obvious.

▶ Use the following questions as your ongoing yardstick.
 – Am I enjoying this – is it exciting and stimulating?
 – Do I feel proud of what we are doing and how we are doing it?
 – Am I learning from what I am doing right now?

The best work is done when we are enjoying ourselves, so being an inspirational manager is a delight all of its own. Therefore being able to answer 'Yes' to these three questions is pivotal to your success.

The reluctant manager

I haven't yet mentioned the reluctant manager, but there are thousands of them out there. Lots of experts are bumped up the promotional ladder via management with little regard for their people skills. Of course they want to progress, so they accept the title and carry on working exactly as they always did. Alternatively, they might be a manager in the making, but no one has told them about the real job and they have been far too busy to find out.

In both situations, reluctant managers focus on the task and people management takes a back seat. As a result, the job becomes overwhelming and dissatisfying. Even if they deliver good results, they are stressed with all the extra pressure. It is a miserable way to spend the week.

If you fall into this camp, imagine coming in on Monday morning just to get on with your own work and have no people management. How would that feel?

▶ If it's a sense of relief, then ask yourself if you really want to be a manager.

▶ If you really hate the idea, you are ready to become an inspirational manager.

This brings us back to Paul Dunmore, at Thomson Directories. When I spoke to Paul's team, they were eager to tell me what a great guy he is. However, they also made it clear that he is not an easy touch – they know they have to perform otherwise they will be sitting down for a tough conversation. At the same time, he is always there to help them sort out difficult situations, keen to celebrate their success and fun to be around. Their mission is to make good money for themselves and deliver in a way that makes him really successful.

If you doubt this description, this book is going to challenge your assumptions about the role of the manager. You will discover that:

▶ you do some things really well

▶ in some areas, you are hopeless

▶ it is the struggles which will make you inspirational.

Welcome to the real world!

There will be lots of ideas that you can adapt to your situation and ways of exploring why you do what you do. The main thing is to join the adventure because inspirational managers are committed to a journey of discovery:

- examining the business and how to make it better
- learning about their teams and how to galvanise them to perform at a high level
- exploration of themselves and how they can improve.

It is possible that you will decide you don't want to be a manager, in which case you can look for the job that really fires you up, which is a great outcome. Alternatively, you might discover that you want nothing more than to see other people thrive.

One last thing to take into account. This is not a 'nice to have' in the twenty-first-century business world – inspirational managers are essential. As Keith Nash, HR Director at Badenoch & Clark, states, 'It's no longer just organisations who demand inspirational managers – it's the employees. Millennials are demanding and need to know they'll be stretched, given their head and treated with respect.'

❝ It's no longer just organisations who demand inspirational managers – it's the employees. ❞

Times are changing and employees are no longer willing to put up with poor management. It is just not acceptable, not least because below par managers are a drain on the organisation. So, following the advice in this book could be your best career move yet!

Summary

▶ People remember inspirational managers. They make a significant impact on people's lives.

▶ Understanding your present style is the best place to start and getting some feedback is a really good way to do this.

▶ Being an inspirational manager requires you to bring your emotions as well as your thoughts to work each day, because it is relationships that make most difference.

▶ Some people manage because it gives them promotion, some enjoy the tactical elements of the work, some are effective in their work, but don't set the world alight. Then there are the inspirational ones.

▶ Enjoying the work, building strong relationships and accepting challenges are good indicators of an inspirational manager.

Action plan

Today

▶ Identify which category of manager sounds like you. Have a think as you go about your day. Are you loving this? If not, what would you love?

Next week

▶ Complete the 360-degree questionnaire yourself (see page 12). If you are feeling brave, ask your manager and some of your team to do it as well.

▶ Note all the feedback and make a plan of what you need to do differently.

Next month

▶ If you have a good relationship with your manager, talk together about how you can begin your development.

▶ If not, identify a mentor or colleagues who want to develop in the same way and agree to support each other.

▶ Work through the book together, discussing the different elements of inspirational management. Practise giving each other straight feedback and use your group to role-play new types of behaviour.

▶ Make sure that you are enjoying yourselves. It is the best indicator!

CHAPTER

3

The beliefs of an inspirational manager

'Don't be rigid, experiment with your own approach and create an environment where other people will experiment too.'

Ian Martin, DTC

Della Garmory at Nationwide believes wholeheartedly in telling the truth and being trustworthy. A high-performing member of her team was delivering great results, but there was no more development she could offer them. Of course, she could have stayed quiet and reaped the benefits by keeping the person within her team, but that would not have sat well with Della's values. Instead she said, 'You've outgrown this job – I can't make it any bigger for you and you've already got enough skills and development for the role. You are brilliant at what you do, so we need to find you a better job outside of the team.'

For some that would feel like professional suicide – why on earth give up such a high performer? But Della knew that she couldn't live with herself if she let the person languish in her team, not to mention the fact that she would probably lose them anyway.

Facing this sort of dilemma clarifies what you really believe in. When the way ahead seems obvious, even when it is not easy, then you understand exactly how important your belief is to you. And in the case of an inspirational manager, it is important to your people too and part of what makes you such a great person to work for. Imagine how valued Della's high performer felt and the comfort it gave the rest of her team to know that she really did have their best interests at heart.

Core beliefs drive us when the chips are down and shine through when fast decisions are needed. Being clear what you believe in means you will have a consistent approach and this is what people trust. Inspirational managers can be relied on to do what they say they will do and that is possible because they have tied their colours to the mast of their core beliefs.

It is a big demand to consistently live these beliefs, but the cost of giving up on them will be even higher. It is a matter of self-respect and if you give that up then others will lose respect for you, too. However much you try to rationalise your behaviour, nothing will really work. You just feel awful, embarrassed or ashamed. My guess is that you can look back and find situations where you felt just like that about yourself – I know I can. Even when the memories are years old, they still have the power to make you cringe. That is because you went against what you believe to be right and you haven't managed to forgive yourself yet.

It is true that beliefs shine through in the tough times, but inspirational managers don't wait for extremis, they live them day by day:

▶ what they say and what they do always matches up

▶ it is a matter of personal pride to be trustworthy

▶ they believe in telling the truth

▶ they want the best for and from their people.

Most important of all, they never compromise on what they believe to be right. In other areas, they will change, listen to other views, alter course and use good ideas from every source, but their values are not for turning! And this is part of what makes them so inspirational.

" Their values are not for turning!"

What inspirational managers believe in

The job of a manager is to work *through* other people, ensuring that they deliver the desired outcomes in a way that is both satisfying for them and productive for the organisation. A bit like being a parent, your job is to help other people grow and discover their strengths and talents. It requires you to make choices – some of them will be tough and some will need to be made so quickly that you will be driven by your instincts rather than rational thought. It is your beliefs that create those instincts and determine which way you jump.

Whatever else they hold dear in their lives, inspirational managers all believe that the only way to deliver top-quality results is by enabling their people to do their best work. This breaks down into some fundamental beliefs that are essential to the job. The essence of being an inspirational manager comes down to believing in and acting on the following core ideas:

- everyone has strengths
- strong relationships support excellence
- tell the truth at all times
- be consistent.

Everyone has strengths

Everyone has strengths they can use in their lives. However hopeless a person may feel, there will always be something that they do really well and it is the manager's job to help them access that strength. Part of what is so exciting about inspirational managers is that they don't believe in underperformance, just the wrong person for the job. Looked at in this way, the task is to find out what the person's strengths are and support their development, but if that doesn't work, to locate the job that will use them to good effect.

" The task is to find out what the person's strengths are and support their development. "

Charlotte Butterfield, at Badenoch & Clark, managed Dave Roberts when he was promoted to a team leader role.

> 'It wasn't an easy move for me and Charlotte had to be brutally honest about my performance, despite my defensiveness. I think I was rather difficult to manage! In time she helped me realise my weaknesses and strengths, but she had to work really hard at it. She used the drip method, bringing in ideas gradually.
>
> If I look back over my appraisals, it was done very subtly – praising the good stuff, highlighting the weak in a way that enabled me to develop. She kept going with this and finally the penny dropped. It took 12 months' discussion and thorough analysis in the 6-month review, one-to-ones, etc., but now I am much more effective with my team.'

Action

▶ Consider how much you believe in people having their own strengths and talents. If you are not sure, look at people in your team and find one thing that you think they are already really good at and one thing you suspect they may be good at.

▶ Think about when you saw another person blossom into a new role or situation. Include yourself by reviewing when you found a new interest or skill that you didn't know you had.

▶ Arrange to talk with your team members to find out what they find most exciting about work and see how you can maximise that energy.

Strong relationships support excellence

The matter of developing excellence is a tough one that will lead other managers to give up or pile on the pressure. Inspirational managers put faith in building strong relationships, because they know we all work hard for those we care about. And as I discovered, when a manager is really positive, people care about them a lot. It creates a virtuous circle – by developing a positive attitude in the team, managers get a positive attitude back and the quality of the work improves.

&& When a manager is really positive, people care about them a lot. It creates a virtuous circle. &&

Pam and Madeline were on their knees after struggling for nine months without appropriate management arrangements due to a radical restructure at Northampton Borough Council. When Fran Rodgers arrived they took to her immediately. Apparently easy-going and laid-back, she was clear about her expectations without being intimidating and always let them know what the priorities were. As a result, their trust began to build and, although the tough job of turning around an ailing service remained, they finally felt that they had the support they needed.

Fran took the time to get to know them all from the outset, rather than just bowing to the exceptionally high demands of the job. She made it clear that she was there for the long haul and determined that they would see it through together. Madeline described her as being 'like an anchor'. Regular one-to-one meetings meant that they always knew they could have quality time with her to talk through their needs and concerns. She is part of the team, but also takes her place as a manager providing them with the support that they need. In this team, more than any other, it is these high levels of trust and strong relationships that will bring them through the difficult challenges ahead.

Action

▶ Think about the relationships that have been most important to you in your working life. How have they affected your attitude to manager–team relationships?

▶ What were the main features of the most positive relationships you have had at work?

▶ Apply those criteria to the relationships you have with your team and consider what you are willing to do to improve them.

Tell the truth at all times

This is a hard belief to abide by, but essential to your development as an inspirational manager. If you want high levels of trust and a team that will deliver exceptional results, they need to know you will tell the truth. When the news is good, this is not a problem, but when the news is tough, strong belief and commitment is what gets you through.

Di missed a deadline at Bromford Housing Group and sat down to talk it through with Helena Moore, her manager. The team approach to an instance such as this is to learn from the experience, so the main thrust of the conversation was about what had happened and what needed to be different next time. Helena believes wholeheartedly in telling the truth in a way that ensures people retain their dignity: 'Always be straightforward. Discuss the issue and be transparent, never mince your words, but then give them time to recover and decide on the next step.'

The conversation was useful for Di and she left knowing how to move forward. Her greatest concern was that she really didn't want to let Helena down: 'I want to deliver because I really want Helena to be successful.' So, there is a paradox. Delivering tough messages doesn't put people off as most of us fear, but, in fact, can make them even more committed. It is when we go through hard times together, that strong relationships are built.

❝ When we go through hard times ... strong relationships are built. ❞

Action

▶ What is your attitude to telling the truth? Do you back off or believe that it is the right thing to do?

▶ Think about a time when you have backed off and notice what the impact was.

▶ Do the same for a time when you told the truth in an effective way and think about the impact on yourself and others. Which one do you feel best about?

Be consistent

This is really important to the people you work with. How the manager behaves determines how other people feel about their working day. It is a tough one to accept because surely everyone is entitled to an off day once in a while? Inspirational managers believe not, or at least that if the off day takes over, then you must acknowledge that you are being a pain and ask for forgiveness. People have to know where they stand. They need to:

▶ know they can trust their manager

▶ understand what will happen when they make a mistake

▶ be able to reach their manager when they need to.

These are fundamental to the development of a safe working environment.

At Data Connection, all work is done out in the open. Nic Larkin expects everyone in his team to talk honestly about what is happening, acknowledge their strengths and weaknesses and to show their work to someone else for comment – and that includes himself. That the team can see these processes adhered to every single day increases the sense of security and trust, which is so important in a high-tech development company like this. Couple this with the fact that Nic sets the tone by owning his own mistakes and you have a team who knows they will get the level of support they need.

Action

▶ What impact did you make when you entered the office this morning? How did your team react?

▶ Do your team know exactly where they stand with you? Do they know for sure that you will support them when the going gets tough? If not, what impact do you think this has?

▶ Think about a manager you have worked for who was totally consistent in their behaviour. What did you take from that and how might you build that into your own management style?

The benefits of being an inspirational manager

Incorporate these beliefs into your daily working life and you will begin to see the benefits of being an inspirational manager. To quote Helena Moore, 'I get personal satisfaction from seeing people develop. There will always be tough times, but the highs outweigh the lows and make it all worthwhile.'

> ❝ I get personal satisfaction from seeing people develop. ... the highs outweigh the lows and make it all worthwhile. ❞

It is a big task to put people first, but there are huge benefits – not least that loyalty levels will go off the scale. When Di told me that she wanted Helena to be successful, it was by no means the first time I had heard that. Teams led by inspirational managers become an inspiration themselves as they:

▶ deliver excellent results

▶ keep developing their strengths

▶ give what it takes to make their manager shine.

As an inspirational manager, you must truly believe in what you do. People have acute radar for a fake, so make sure that you demonstrate your passion and commitment. Take Ben Lee, at Mace, an ex-brickie foreman who specialises in highly colourful language and attitude to match. There is no way that anything other than the real thing will get past him.

Ben Wood, his manager, was leading a project team for Heathrow Terminal Five. Despite Ben Lee's flamboyant style, Ben Wood saw his potential and wanted him to flourish. He also wanted to retain that energy, albeit it cleaned up a bit, because he realised just how much could be achieved. Ben Lee was very straightforward and a quick learner, so it didn't take him long to pick up on the encouragement to 'stop shouting!'.

As a result, he did some great work with the architect, has become a friend and support to Ben Wood and begun raising his profile with other managers and directors. It was that inspirational manager ability to recognise a diamond in the rough that allowed Ben Lee's spirit and spark to be channelled for the good of the team, the business and both Bens.

Managing upwards in an inspirational way

So far, we have talked about managing your own team, but how does it work when you are managing upwards? This brings us into the realms of organisational values and the prevailing management approach.

Organisational values

If you are fortunate, you will work in an organisation that places a high value on the development of talent and believes in being honest, consistent and trustworthy. It will make your job so much easier because you won't be working against the grain and will receive all the support you need to lead your team in an inspirational way.

If, on the other hand, the business values different things, you have to decide how you will manage it. You have a number of choices.

▶ Hold to your own beliefs and build a strong, inspirational team. As soon as you can, make it clear what you are doing and encourage others to join you. In time, as results show the impact of a people-centred approach to management, you may find that you can share your ideas and beliefs more widely in the organisation.

▶ If you are in a changing culture, look for other managers who are keen to change alongside you. The more support you have at this stage the better. Beliefs and attitudes don't change overnight and everyone needs consistent challenge to be the best they can be. Talk about successes, but talk about failures, too – remember, that is where most learning will come from.

▶ If the difference between you and others is too wide and you can see no way to exert your influence or to work in the way that you believe to be right, then you have to make choices. It may sound drastic, but all you can do is leave or decide to stay and risk being unhappy.

Supporting a new culture

Ian Martin, a manager at the Diamond Trading Company (DTC, part of the De Beers group), was tasked with pulling together a team to build a new model for pricing diamonds. It was a pretty daunting prospect at the outset, but he was clear that he wanted not only to develop the product but also a strong team of people who would build on each other's strengths. De Beers has a long history of looking after its employees, but the culture is now changing to be more dynamic and challenging, so Ian had a great opportunity to develop his own style of inspirational management.

He was also supported by the company's vision: 'to make people feel like jewels'. This translated into valuing people, showing appreciation and nurturing talent by giving responsibility and accountability. It was a great backdrop for Ian's teambuilding work.

Ian's beliefs are definitely those of an inspirational manager, but the previous business style hadn't given him the space or opportunity to develop his skills with people. Working together in a coaching relationship, Ian and I explored the challenges ahead, the right people for the team and the best way to go about developing them. Once he had pulled together the people he wanted, we all spent a day together understanding what the new company values meant to them as a team. We had a great time and lots of fun:

▶ learning more about each other

▶ understanding strengths and development areas

▶ learning a bit about life outside work

▶ setting some clear ground rules for team behaviour.

Then began the task of holding to the ground rules and delivering on expectations. Our coaching discussions supported Ian in defining his management style and navigating tough times. When you are working in a changing culture, support levels for the new ways aren't always high, so it really helps to know that someone else believes in the same things.

Ian followed his heart, held to his beliefs and began the task of balancing support with dynamic challenge. His aim was for a team who confronted inappropriate behaviour – he knew that if they felt safe enough to do that, they would also feel free to be creative. He realised that the first step was to let them know how much they were appreciated. 'If you give positive feedback often enough, then constructive criticism is much easier to hear.' True enough, he now has people who will listen to feedback without being defensive. It doesn't mean that they are perfect or that they are working to their optimum yet, but it does mean there's a better chance of learning and high performance.

❝ If you give positive feedback often enough, then constructive criticism is much easier to hear. ❞

Managing your manager

Your own manager will have an influence on what you can do with your own team, so building a strong relationship with them will free you up to be as inspirational as you wish.

All the managers I spoke to had equally inspirational managers above them, which makes their task significantly easier since their reporting relationship matches those core beliefs. Tesh Kataria, at Tower Homes, is fortunate to be managed by Stacey Mitchell, who believes that it is really important to know her people well. Her two direct reports are totally different and she has to be able to hold them both to task. She sets out to understand their motivation, be clear what makes them tick and know enough about their personal lives to be able to take it into account when necessary so she:

- understands how energetic Tesh is, but is able to step back to look at things objectively
- doesn't want to demoralise him, so seeks a balance of support and challenge and accepts that there will be mistakes
- knows that he is quite happy to hear critical feedback
- ensures that they talk on a regular basis to catch up with what he is doing and offer help.

Stacey's other direct report is more like she is herself – sensitive and self-critical – so giving her tough feedback is a much more delicate job. By using her knowledge and understanding of them both, she can do it in the best way possible to ensure top-quality results all round.

If you don't work for an inspirational manager, then you have a more difficult task on your hands. The key factor is not to let it change how you want to work yourself. You have direct experience of not being cared for and developed in the way that you believe to be your due, so let it increase your commitment to your own people. If the lack of inspiration is a problem for you, look for a mentor in the workplace. There are sure to be other inspirational managers you can relate to and use as a role model.

Become an inspiration to your own manager.

Sticking to your guns may also mean that you become an inspiration to your own manager. A lot of people only have role models of autocratic or laissez-faire managers to go on, so if you have a great team and deliver strong results, they will inevitably notice what you are doing. Always hold to your beliefs:

- trust to strengths
- build the relationship
- tell the truth.
- be consistent

You will soon find that change begins to happen in front of your eyes.

Summary

▶ Inspirational managers have core beliefs that centre on people and their development.

▶ They believe that everyone has their own particular strengths and given the necessary support, they can develop them.

▶ By building strong relationships, they create a working environment where people can come into their own.

▶ Telling the truth at all times means that trust levels are high in the team and everyone knows where they stand.

▶ Consistent behaviour means people always know where they stand.

▶ There are significant pay-offs for working in this way that will be appreciated and rewarded by the organisation and people alike.

▶ If you can find a way to work with the organisation's values, it makes life easier. If it is not possible, you have to decide if there is space for you to work in the way you want to.

▶ If your own manager doesn't have the same core beliefs, don't give up. Instead, see if you can inspire them, too.

Action plan

Today

▶ Consider how you manage at the moment and see if you can identify the beliefs that underpin your style.

▶ As you do this, think about whether or not they are beliefs that make the most of your people.

Next week

▶ Take one inspirational manager belief a day and work to it to see what difference it makes to your team.

▶ Make notes about how this changes your impact.

▶ Ask for feedback from your team members at the end of the week to explore any differences that they experienced.

Next month

▶ Talk to your colleagues and find the people who are keen to develop their own inspirational beliefs. Share your thinking with them and find ways in which you can support each other.

▶ Get feedback on specific issues from supportive colleagues who will be with you in meetings. Take five minutes at the end of each meeting to share some feedback.

▶ Take the feedback to heart and act on it over the next couple of days and see what effect it has.

▶ Once you are clear on your beliefs as an inspirational manager, talk about them to others, including your own direct line manager. Doing this will help you stick to your beliefs in the long term.

CHAPTER 4

Keep on learning

'Don't get it into your head that being a manager makes you superior. Put your people up there instead, then do what it takes to get the best out of them.'

Tesh Kataria, Tower Homes

Isn't it interesting that the best people are often the most self-effacing? They are the least likely to say, 'I'm really good at this' and quick to tell you where they could do better. This is exactly what happened when I met Paul Dunmore, at Thomson Directories. While telling me what he does to ease the tedium of constant outbound calls, he suddenly stopped and said, 'Talking now, I realise I've become complacent recently. I haven't been doing enough to brighten their day. I really must get moving again.' Because the realisation was so important, he shared it rather than keeping quiet, despite the fact that he was being interviewed.

Inspirational managers make a point of nurturing their curiosity and constantly seeking the next challenge and learning. However long they have been managing people they recognise that there will always be something they don't know or some way they can improve. Whether in their area of skill, the business, the people they work with or themselves, they want to explore next steps, understand more and push the boundaries. So being an inspirational manager requires you to remain open to change at all times – in fact, to actively seek it out!

66 *Being an inspirational manager requires you to remain open to change.* 99

This might feel like a pretty unwelcome addition if you are under the cosh with loads of deadlines to deliver and it is true that it takes time and commitment. However the learning will come from *how* you deliver and meet the deadlines and what you do to support your team. You don't have to do much extra, just pay close attention to how you do the day job.

The value of self-criticism

'Management comes from passion. I'm always thinking how I can do things better and I'm never too proud to admit I'm wrong.' So says Charlotte Butterfield, at Badenoch & Clark. She has a real drive to improve and is determined to be top of her game. Her biggest fear is complacency: 'I need that slight fear factor – it leads me to give the extra 1 per cent. I need to know others are better than me. To be truly good, I must be self-critical – that's the only way I'll improve on a regular basis.'

This is the drive of an inspirational manager. You can never let up. Your people will fluctuate all the time – their challenges change, they go through mood swings and they grow – so you must always be one step ahead.

For some it is hard to be self-critical, but it is really the only way to keep improving. According to Charlotte, 'I was no good at the outset. I was too tough and pretty brutal at times. I had to develop a soft side. I can't bear to be bad at stuff, so I ask advice whenever I need it.'

She learned a lot from her first team. They were too ambitious for her to manage and she really struggled. She did her best, but that combination of an ambitious team and her being too junior a manager led to loss of respect all round. At first glance, it looked as though she would never make it, but that striving quality gave her the edge and she was determined to make the most of the learning opportunity.

Charlotte described how her manager, Alison, 'helped get me out of being rubbish'. She was a constant source of support over four years, working with Charlotte in a coaching style to help her think through the implications of her behaviour and the most likely impact on the team. Eventually she was moved out to lead another team, but she believes that 'it was good for me to struggle. It made me work hard and think through how to change.'

The end result? Charlotte has gone from being a 'doubtful' to winning the award for Manager of the Year at Badenoch & Clark. All because she refused to give up, looked for the learning and acted on it.

Developing your emotional muscle

Inspirational managers spend a lot of time working their emotional muscle – this is a big part of what makes them so special. Emotions are key to effective relationships and effective relationships deliver the best results. People who feel valued, excited and stimulated do great work and that is good for the team and the organisation.

“ Emotions are key to effective relationships. ”

Understanding yourself

The first steps in honing that emotional muscle require you to understand your significant behaviour patterns:

▶ the drivers that help you make the most of your skills and talents and ensure you use them to good effect

▶ the occasions that stop you in your tracks. We all do our own version of a tantrum at times and different triggers will get us there in seconds, but, as soon as you know what those triggers are, then you are in with a chance of avoiding them.

Before Paul Dunmore came to Thomson Directories, he owned and ran two fruit and veg. shops. It was loads of fun, but extremely stressful. Working daily with perishable food means that life and profit become very immediate – your stock simply rots if you don't sell it in time. It was only when he left his young helper in charge that he realised just how much he was trying to keep control. Sure that his way was right, he was infuriated to see that stock had been moved while he was away. Early mornings, the stress of the work and an assumption that he knew best led Paul to shout at his assistant, but he did leave everything where it was for that day. 'We sold more than ever before, so I learned a lot about myself, and about placing stock, from that 16-year-old.'

Everyone has those moments when they lose control because the world is not cooperating with them – even inspirational managers. The difference is that they will ponder on what happened and see what they can learn for the future. So Paul learned not to assume that he always knows the right way to do things, not to stereotype people – 16-year-olds can have great ideas – and that stress will bring out different behaviour in him.

Action

Choose one of your habitual behaviour patterns – something that others would recognise as typical of you.

▶ Write down examples of where the behaviour works and what it achieves.

▶ Think about times when it hasn't worked. Make a list of occasions and note both the immediate impact and long-term effect.

▶ Think about how it serves you to behave that way – that is, what it enables you to continue doing/thinking about the world around you. For example, always believing that you are right means you don't have to question yourself, which feels safe.

▶ Take one situation and think about other ways to handle it. If you get stuck, consider how others would respond to the same situation.

▶ Experiment with using some of the alternatives and see what the reactions are.

▶ Think about these reactions and what you learn from them. Is your behaviour pattern still the right thing to do and, if yes, why? If not, why not and what have you learned that will help you work better in the future?

Working through situations in this way extends your thinking and understanding of the world around you. By considering your impact, you see yourself through someone else's eyes, which can be both fascinating and uncomfortable. Understanding the benefit of the behaviour – the way it helps you to feel positive, righteous or justified, for example – will give you more insight into what drives you day by day.

Understanding others

Your emotional muscle will improve your sensitivity to others, making relationships much easier, but you need to keep using it or the muscle will waste away.

Seeing the world through another person's eyes helps you understand:

- why people are affected in the way that they are
- what they need in order to move forward in a positive way
- how to help them learn from a situation.

However fine-tuned your sensitivity, you won't always be correct in your assumptions. The trick is to recognise this and be honest about it. What matters to people is not that you are always right, but that you have taken time to think about the situation from their perspective and that you want to understand. Once you have achieved this kind of relationship, then every struggle or success is fodder for improvement.

What matters . . . is . . . that you want to understand.

Complacency is the big problem as Chris Hiles discovered. He had five great managers in the Leeds office of Thomson Directories, Paul Dunmore included, and they had a reputation for being the highest-performing office in the company. Then their results dropped. They had all become too satisfied, including Chris. Since then he has learned, 'never buy into your own press. Management is a never-ending journey.' Taking your eye off the ball, even for a short space of time, is a recipe for disaster.

Action

- Make time when people want to speak with you. If you are not sure what they are saying, summarise your understanding. This will invite them to clarify and make it clear that you are listening, so there is more chance they will take a risk and speak openly. (See also Chapter 6.)

- If you suspect that the most important thing is not being said, try it out. For example, say, 'I was just thinking about . . . and wondered if it's important to you?' If they don't agree, just give it up and move on, but it is worth a try.

- Do *not* try to be an amateur psychologist – it will only put them off. If you are concerned about something, be open about it and say so. If you think they might be concerned, ask.

- At the end of each discussion, think about what was going on. Consider the messages you took away from the meeting and then ▶

---

listen to your own feelings to see if you sensed anything that was not being said. Keep this information in mind as you work with the person and pay attention to their needs.

Nature or nurture?

Is it something I can learn to do or do I have to be born an inspirational manager? Is it a question of nature or nurture?

On the side of nature, some of us do have natural people skills. Those who are essentially extroverted, for example, will find it much easier to walk around the office having a quick chat with random people. They will also love the sociable side of management, thinking of quirky ways to bring people together to have fun. Allison Nicoll, at Freedom Finance is like that. Naturally creative, she loves to think up new incentives and ideas for fun rewards. An ideal skill for a manager in an outbound call centre.

There are also people who have an innate understanding and fascination about people and what drives them. This makes management an ideal job and they will thrive in a team environment. Tesh Kataria at Tower Homes is a perfect example. He finds people appealing, wants to know what makes them tick and what will make them feel happy. It is part of who he is, so is no real effort. It's a talent that can lead to strong relationships, a drive to see other people succeed and achieve great results.

But what if you are stronger on a rational level and prefer your own company or that of a few special friends? Is it possible to nurture your management ability? Do you have to become a lively, creative, sociable animal in order to build a great team? No, you just have to find your own style.

Again, there is a comparison with parenting. We all do it in different ways with varying degrees of success. If you are willing to stretch yourself into new areas of learning, you can develop your own version of being an inspirational manager. This is key – don't expect yourself to be like Allison or Tesh, you have to find your own way. You may be much quieter, taking people on one side to say thank you, rather than going to the pub. You may need to access the creativity of your team if it doesn't come naturally to you. Whatever you do, your way will be just as good as another. ➤

We are all different and the trick is to make the most of your strengths and reduce the impact of your weaknesses.

I worked with a manager who was excellent with people, but totally hopeless at planning. There were two options: learn more about planning or partner with someone who is already good at it. This is an interesting judgement call for every developing manager, whether a natural or not. No one has every skill required for the job. You will do some things right, courtesy of Mother Nature, others you will have to nurture through development and training. If you are interested and want to learn, then you can nurture that side of yourself. If not, then the best option may be to partner with someone who is a natural. Inspirational managers do what it takes to get the best from their people, but no one said you had to do it all yourself, just see that it all gets done.

Where will I find this learning?

Aside from formal learning, you will gain most by paying attention to the lessons that are all around you hence that hackneyed phrase, 'the university of life'. Becoming an inspirational manager is the equivalent of doing a masters degree in people, so take your lessons wherever you find them:

- ▶ family and friends
- ▶ colleagues
- ▶ chosen role models.

Learning from family and friends

For managers, being around any people is a source of learning. Of course, your team will teach you masses, but they are not the only ones. Family and close friends are great teachers – *they* won't let you off the hook because they are afraid of a poor appraisal! The trick is to listen, especially when you want to defend like mad, because it is probably exactly the message you *need* to hear.

Whenever I do 360-degree feedback work with managers and leaders, I always ask if they have shown the report to their partner, a close friend or family. When they have, I can guarantee that the partner recognised all the feedback – often saying, 'I could have told you that for free!' So, listening to feedback from friends and family is not just good for those relationships, it will be good for your management style, too. These people see you at your best and worst, so pay attention and you will learn a huge amount.

Ben Wood, at Mace, learned a lesson just by having his first child. Once he was a family man, he realised that he had never done enough to include families – it had just never occurred to him. However much people tell you things, you may never get to grips with them until they impinge directly on you. A bit of personal experience is a great driver.

Action

▶ Talk to your partner or closest friend about the behaviour patterns you see in yourself and ask how they experience you.

▶ Try out new behaviours with close friends and family and ask them to give you feedback. This gives you a safe start as you make your first attempts.

▶ Ask them to point out your blind spots so that you can build these into your awareness.

Peoplewatching

Experiment next time you go to a shopping mall. Find a comfortable place for a coffee that gives you a clear view of people walking by. Then, just watch:

▶ Notice your assumptions about the expressions on faces – the people you assume are happy and those who look miserable.

▶ Look at their posture/dress, listen to the tone of their voices, if you can hear – how do you imagine they feel? Do you think that they are happy, sad, switched off, depressed?

▶ Choose someone who really catches your eye. Imagine yourself in their place and have a play with what life might be like. If you were in their shoes, what do you think the problems and delights might be?

> ▶ Notice how people relate to each other. Do people sitting in the café around you talk to each other? How do their faces change as they do so? Which do you think are angry, in love, just needing to get out of the house?
>
> ▶ How might you look to other people? Would they be interested to know more about you or would they rather go to the dentist? Do you make enough effort to appeal to others or do you expect them to take you as they find you?
>
> This is a really useful exercise and one that is worth repeating regularly. It is all about developing your emotional muscle. As you increase your interest in people, you will get better at reading them and it will impact on your relationships in the workplace.

Learning from colleagues

You will learn a lot from talking to colleagues and sharing experiences. This is particularly important for new managers because it can be lonely when you have your first team. Inspirational managers remember the confusion of those early days and are always willing to support their new colleagues. So think about getting together with other managers for discussion, listening to speakers or getting yourself a mentor – whatever it is that you need.

> 66 *Inspirational managers remember the confusion of those early days.* 99

You would also do well to find the experts in your organisation because a robust network of them will be one of your greatest treasures. This is particularly helpful when you realise that all the best ideas are nicked!

Paul Dunmore learned that last lesson from the Beatles:

'Daft as it sounds, I saw a quote by John Lennon: "We don't have an original bone in our bodies. We just go out and listen to Buddy Holly or Elvis, take out the bits we like, put them all together and that's what makes the Beatles. So go on, copy everyone." I thought, that's what I need to do in Sales. I need to watch all those people in Sales and copy what they do. So I looked at the league table to find the best people and watched what they did and they were all kind enough to let me – I sold them the idea and they said yes. Then, lo and behold, in six months I was the top salesperson and all I'd done was pick the best bits of what they did. I remember, they asked me to do a presentation and these four

Action
- Identify the inspirational managers in your organisation and see what they do, then try it on for size.
- Next time you are unsure or have a problem, seek out someone other than your manager and talk it through to see what you can learn.
- Arrange to get together with other managers and talk about your learning. Be clear that this is about pinching each other's best ideas and set the tone by being generous yourself!

blokes stood there with their mouths agape. I've always been grateful, so I realised that I need to help others when they're struggling.'

Learning from chosen role models

All of this leads us on to the idea of role models. You will have one, even if you have never thought it through consciously. It may be someone who has managed you in the past or someone from another part of your life.

For Della, at Nationwide, it was her father. He worked his way up through the ranks in the textile industry, handling a tough shift pattern and studying in the evenings. She has clear memories of answering the door to people who worked for him, wanting advice and guidance at any time of the day or night, and he never turned them away. It was obvious to Della that her father was a well-respected manager and his ability to build relationships at all levels was something that she admired and still does to this day. It is not surprising, then, that relationship with people has always been very important to Della, both inside and outside of work.

Interestingly, his father was also the role model for Tesh Kataria at Tower Homes. His dad had his own menswear retail business and Tesh was expected to work there every Saturday, even though he hated it. He suffered it for ten years, but realises now that it provided him with a basic education in selling. His mother added an interesting dimension by modelling the Asian way of showing respect to your elders and family. She always put the family first and, while we were talking, he realised that is exactly what he does now with his team.

So, who are your role models? There may be one person who has had an impact on you over many years that you still emulate. Alternatively, you

---

Action

▶ Identify the people who have had the most influence on your life. How are you like them now and what have you taken from their example?

▶ Think about what you *don't* like in your role model, then make a quick and honest check to see if you have adopted those traits yourself.

▶ List the assumptions your role model leads you to make – that is, those things you take for granted or automatically assume to be true. Read back through the list and decide which ones work well for you and which are holding you up.

▶ At your next team meeting, notice how these assumptions work in practice. Make a plan for any changes that you want to put in place.

---

may find that you have a negative role model – someone you know you *never* want to be like. Experiencing bad behaviour first hand is a great spur to change, making you determined never to wreak the same havoc on other people.

Yourself as a role model

Of course, it isn't only about your role models but also who takes you on as theirs! It could be happening right now – someone will be looking at you and thinking, 'That's how management should be done' or worse, 'I never want to manage people in that way.'

I once worked with a manager who had the latter impact on his team. So determined was he to be right that there was no space for anyone else to shine. He kept HR busy recruiting as talented people left, vowing never to work with someone like that again. On the other hand, it can make a really powerful contribution to the development of people – a bit like aversion therapy. A really negative boss has driven a number of the managers mentioned in this book towards a positive management style. Those struggles have done a lot to fuel their passion for inspirational management.

We need to build a new role model for management and say goodbye to:

▶ managers who do the work themselves

▶ authoritarian managers who demand obedience

▶ overly pliable managers who are afraid to tell the truth.

Management is not a soft option. It is a job that requires real courage, commitment and dedication in its own right.

It is exciting to be a manager at a time like this when a new way is being created. You have the chance to mould what others expect and want to be.

Summary

▶ Inspirational managers keep learning – it is what makes them so good at their job.

▶ Learning about yourself will help you to understand other people better.

▶ Develop your radar for understanding others and your work will be much more effective.

▶ Some of being an inspirational manager will come to you naturally; some you will have to learn. If you are willing and open to change, there is no reason why you shouldn't do it.

▶ You can gain learning from a number of places – family, business, colleagues and role models.

Action plan
Today

▶ Work out what you have learned over the past week. Identify how you have used it and how it will be useful in the future.

▶ Be aware through the day how you come across. What kind of role model are you to others? At the end of the day, make a note of what you have learned from the exercise.

Next week

▶ Explore the possibility of using 360-degree feedback to find out more about your impact with your team and colleagues. Ask HR to help you find a coach or a mentor to talk through the results.

▶ Think about how you trip yourself up and the impact it has. If you don't know, ask colleagues or team members for feedback and be open to hearing what they say.

Next month

▶ Set up a learning group with colleagues who also want to build their emotional muscle. Have each person talk through a specific work issue and the others in the group help them explore it by means of coaching and feedback.

▶ Arrange to meet once a month to learn together.

▶ If you need more information about learning sets, ask your HR department or read a suitable book (see Appendix 2 for some pointers).

CHAPTER 5

Focusing your attention

'You can't complain any more – it's not what you are paid for!'

Alan Bishop, COI

The ideal manager is one who has drive and ambition without too much ego. As Alan Bishop, at COI, acknowledges, 'These are contradictory qualities, so, if you find these special people, treasure them.' He is right, it is a rare combination, but an ideal one for a manager. Drive and ambition keep you striving for strong results and appropriate levels of ego mean that you won't buy into your own publicity and think you have done it all on your own.

Inspirational managers make a conscious effort to hold both these qualities in balance. By focusing on the team and the business, they can drive for results as well as stretch talent, giving the organisation a pipeline of great people ready for the next challenge. However, they also focus attention on themselves, not just to polish their haloes, but to make sure that they are in good shape to do the job. Managers who feel undervalued, exhausted or limited by their bosses will have difficulty giving real attention to their own teams.

When the balance is lost in either direction, problems occur. Managers will work well enough, but may not deliver the exceptional results of an inspirational manager – and they certainly won't have people queuing up to join their teams.

Why focus matters

There are two main areas of focus:

▶ Focusing attention on yourself means taking care of your health, your own career and your work–home balance, all of which ensures that you can deliver good work

▶ Focusing primarily on others requires you to pay attention to what they need from you and do your best to deliver it, so that they can do their best work.

Getting the balance right

The ideal is a balance of the two (Figure 5.1). Just as it is important to understand yourself if you want to understand others, so it is important to take care of yourself if you want to do your best for others. You won't manage your team well if you are exhausted or distracted. If you feel well rested and supported by your own manager and peers, then you will have the right levels of attention and energy to give to your team.

❝ Just as it is important to understand yourself if you want to understand others, so it is important to take care of yourself if you want to do your best for others. ❞

Once the balance is right, a virtuous, reinforcing circle begins to spin, encouraging relationships to grow. Because managers feel positive about themselves, they give attention to other people, who give them positive feedback and appreciation, which builds their self-esteem, making it easier to focus on other people ... The result is robust relationships based on mutual respect, support and trust.

❝ The result is robust relationships based on mutual respect, support and trust. ❞

You will read stories that reflect this cycle throughout the book. Stories about managers who do all they can to get the best from and for their people, but not at the expense of themselves. They know that their mood will impact on their team, so speak out if they don't get the support they need from their own manager or believe something is not right or fair. And they tend to their own careers to make sure that they are always challenged

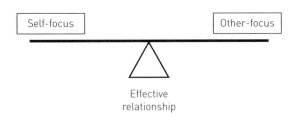

Figure 5.1 Getting the balance right

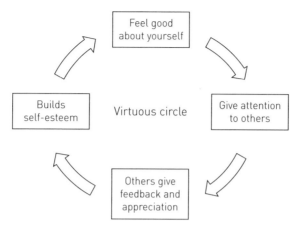

Figure 5.2 Virtuous circle

and excited about the job, thereby setting a great role model for budding managers around them.

Focusing attention on yourself

You can't look after anyone else effectively until you look after yourself. Just think of those days when you go in to work feeling exhausted or down-hearted. You may have slept badly or had a depressing day yesterday, so all you want to do is hide away, lock the door and be left alone. Compare that to a day when you feel bright, energetic and ready to go. My guess is that you are much more productive and effective in everything you do on these days.

However well you look after yourself, you will still have down days, but paying attention to yourself and your own needs does prepare you to handle the impact. It also helps you to take seriously times when you need support or help with a tough situation or difficult person.

Action

As an inspirational manager who takes good care of yourself, you will do the following.

▶ Build a development plan with your manager so that you get

---

the support and challenge you need to keep up your standard of work.

▶ Inform the relevant people about your career aspirations and make sure that they know of your achievements. If you have no desire for further promotion, think about how you can stay fresh and retain your enjoyment in your present job.

▶ Find yourself a mentor or coach to help you understand how to improve your performance. Not only will this be a huge help to you, but you will really enjoy having the undivided attention of another person for a while.

▶ Build a network of colleagues who think in a similar way so that you always have a port of call in a storm and someone to talk to when you need it.

▶ Work out the right balance between home and work so that you don't feel resentful about the amount of time you give to the workplace. Once you have worked it out, do all you can to stick to it.

Focusing on other people

The ability to do this effectively is central to the art of management. Your job is to deliver great results for the business by enabling your people to do their best work. You will achieve this if you have positive and respectful relationships. If you think of a time when you felt undervalued and the impact it had on your work, then you will understand why this is so important to your team.

For inspirational managers, it is also what makes the job so satisfying and rewarding. That ability to connect with other people in a way that ensures they make the best of themselves is a delight and brings real appreciation from all sides. It may mean devoting time and attention to others, but it is exciting and deeply satisfying.

Action

Begin now to focus as an inspirational manager so that you:

▶ Take care to choose people who have the skills and abilities you need, who suit the team and who you can make a commitment to. ➤

> ▶ Give your management tasks priority, never skimping on one-to-one time, following up on what has been agreed and always checking how you can help someone who is not on form.
>
> ▶ Make your expertise known outside your own team, so that others can ask for help and you can ask them when they have the skills you need.
>
> ▶ Know your people and let them know you, being clear that this is not a traditional friendship. Your direct reports need to know that you will take control, set boundaries and hold them to task as appropriate.
>
> ▶ Resolve always to tell the truth so that people know exactly where they stand and do it in a way that leaves people feeling valued and able to move forward.
>
> ▶ Provide a positive presence in the office. Emotions are contagious, so how you behave will affect how everyone else feels. If you feel dreadful, have had the night from hell or just need time to concentrate on a piece of work, let people know what is happening. Don't leave them to guess or they will imagine the worst.

What about my own work?

If you want to be an inspirational manager, you can't afford to focus entirely on your own results. As soon as you take on the job of being a manager, you step back from the centre of attention. It is really interesting – for your team, you are the prime person, so very important, but, if you get carried away with it, you will be in trouble. As Nic Larkin, at Data Connection, says, 'Don't think about being the boss – you're not an authority, your sphere of operation is just different from theirs.'

It is a delicate balance to hold. Your people want to know that you are in control, that you have a clear vision of where the team is going and you will fight their corner. On the other hand, the more you take your place within the team, the better the relationships will be. You will only manage all this if you are clear what is important to you and that requires you to focus on yourself for long enough to understand.

Taking care of yourself will impact directly on the well-being of the team. Mick Kent, CEO of Bromford Housing Group, says that how he enters the office will determine 'whether it's summer or winter that day'. On the other hand, you need to focus attention on what your people need and how they are doing with their work. Taking time in the morning to say 'Hello', remembering what is happening in their lives and giving clear and regular feedback will ensure that they feel valued and respected by you. And this is a major contributor to achieving high levels of performance.

Identifying your natural focus

To clarify where your present focus is, answer the following questions quickly, without giving them too much thought.

▶ Consider what you expect from the people around you. Is it their job to serve you or vice versa? How much time do you spend with them during the working day?

▶ If there is a choice between your needs and those of another person, which way do you go?

▶ What is the factor most likely to deliver in terms of results – time to concentrate or working with others?

▶ When something goes wrong in your team, where do you place responsibility?

▶ Is it important for you to bounce ideas off other people or do you prefer to work things out on your own?

If your answers are clear-cut in one direction, then you are probably a bit out of balance. Ideally, you will respond to most of the questions with 'it depends' and you will see a case for all the options. Nothing in human relationships is straightforward, so the ability to vary the direction of your focus is a great asset. You need the inputs of others to give life colour and energy. Add in some time on your own to think about your own needs, complete your own work and think ahead to what the team needs and you have the perfect balance.

Seeing the world through another set of eyes

Allison Nicoll, at Freedom Finance, managed a person who didn't find it easy to join in with the daily banter of a thriving call centre team. Doing really well in everything except this area of communication, she wanted to find a way to help him come out of himself more. The standard interventions had been of little help, so Allison took the time to consider what the issue actually was.

She realised that he was a quiet and shy person, unable at that point to come out of his shell. She also suspected that the jacket he habitually wore represented that shell.

Using the stimulus of an exceptionally hot summer's day, she suggested that he might take the jacket off to be cooler. He was horrified and owned up that it was his protection – a very brave statement in the circumstances.

Allison saw this as a breakthrough and wanted to go a bit further. Her idea was very insightful. She suggested that they make a pact: if he took off his jacket, she would wear a different outfit to work. A regular trouser wearer, she knew that if she wore a skirt, it would draw so much attention that no one would notice the loss of his jacket! He also realised that it was a big ask for her, so it was a clear statement that she was in this with him.

They each kept their side of the agreement and, sure enough, there was much ribaldry about the skirt! The experience of taking off his 'protective' jacket helped him take a further risk and he developed a real alliance with the loudest member of the team – both unsure in their own ways. Allison told me that if ever they had to break up the team, she would want to leave these two together as they are such a good foil for each other.

Helping people make the best of themselves is never straightforward and can take time and subtlety to achieve. This situation required Allison to focus attention on her direct report to work out what the issue really was. Her solution was driven by her ability to put herself in his place – something that takes a great deal of self-awareness and focus to achieve. As a result of her balanced focus, she was able to deliver an innovative and creative solution that led to a real result.

Crisis of focus

As with everything, it is easy for the scales to tip and, when they stay that way, it creates real problems for a manager, leading to either:

- ▶ excessive focus on others, which can lead to stress and burnout
- ▶ excessive focus on yourself, which can lead to bullying and extreme upward management.

Excessive focus on others

When the scales tip over into a concentration of care for others, the problems are tough (Figure 5.3).

As an other-focused manager, placing all your attention on another person to the exclusion of yourself may feel positive to begin with, but the feeling won't last. When all your energy goes into pleasing and placating, the team soon loses confidence. It never works. You go one down in their estimation and they will look elsewhere for support, guidance and reassurance. Inevitably, relationships suffer, because a team needs to see their manager as strong.

Stacey Mitchell, at Tower Homes, had a moment of being other-focused when Tesh Kataria came to her full of enthusiasm about sending personal letters as part of a marketing campaign, rather than the traditional glossy brochure. She let herself get overtaken by his energy, but later realised that they had both missed some vital information out of the letter. Consequently, they received a huge response, but not from the people they were trying to target. It was great learning for her, especially when managing such a

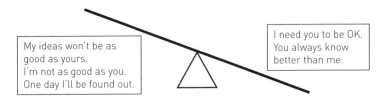

Figure 5.3 Excessive focus on others

dynamic and energetic manager. It was clear that she had been drawn into the concept without checking the detail. Since then, she has made a point of always taking a step back in order to avoid letting her balance of focus slip so totally on to the other.

The desire to keep people happy makes it tempting to dismiss personal concerns and it becomes chronic when someone feels out of their depth. The ploy may work if you have a boss who likes to keep control of the detail. All you have to do is pander to their every whim and give them exactly what they ask for and they will be happy. However, if you happen on a boss who expects you to do your own job, life will become extremely uncomfortable.

Action

▶ Sit down with a notebook and draw a map of the most important people in your work area at the moment. Do it quickly without giving it too much thought.

▶ Write the status or title against each name. Consider the influence each person has, write down why you think you need to please them and what the risk is if you don't.

▶ Now imagine that you are a totally independent person. Do you think that the reasoning is right?

▶ If so, make a note of how you can reduce the risks to a reasonable level. If the perceived risks are out of proportion, write a clear list of the reality. Keep the list so you can refer back to it next time you feel anxious.

In fact, your biggest risk may well come from being too tentative. If your manager has faith in your ability to deliver, perhaps it is time to believe them and trust yourself. If that feels too hard, talk with your manager about some coaching or mentoring, so that you can get another perspective on the job and your capabilities.

Stress

Workplace stress is an issue that has been much studied and, if you think you are suffering excessively, then please seek help straight away. This is not something to be stoic about – do what you need to in order to feel better.

Some people thrive on a bit of 'healthy' stress – all that adrenalin running up to a deadline and a sense of satisfaction when the work is completed can be quite exciting. The issue is whether or not you are choosing the stress from a place of balanced focus – that is, you know the excessive amount of work you are doing will be short-lived and you decide it is worth putting in the extra effort, so you actively put aside your self-focus to go with the demands of the business.

Problems occur when you become overly focused on the needs of others and the business to the detriment of yourself. Then you feel compelled to put aside personal needs in order to answer the demands of your job. This adrenalin *doesn't* feel good – it builds up and takes you into overdrive, so you lose your sense of proportion and feel entirely at the behest of other people.

Action

If you manage to spot this happening in yourself, act quickly to redress the balance.

▶ Find a quiet place and let people know that you are not to be interrupted for an hour.

▶ Make a list of all the demands on your time and give a score out of ten for the level of stress of each one.

▶ For those of low stress, consider which ones can be put on hold for a time or handed to someone in your team or a colleague.

▶ For the high-stress areas of your work, give some thought to why they are so stressful.

  – Who is making the demands?

  – Who are you afraid of letting down?

  – What is the risk of saying no or changing the deadlines?

▶ As soon as possible, speak to your manager about the help you need, being clear that working this way is not sustainable. If your manager is the one you are afraid to disappoint, talk it through with a colleague or coach to prepare for the meeting.

Burnout

You know your focus on others has gone off the scale when you enter burnout. You will recognise this if:

- You are working long hours, losing sleep, but still feel that you are not making any progress
- You hate the idea of going to work in the morning
- You feel down and depressed, with no energy or enthusiasm for things that previously excited you
- You have lost sight of your own needs.

By this point, you are so used to putting other people before yourself that it is hard to believe there is any other way to behave. It is easy to see how this happens when people have a vocation – helping others is good work to do, but it also invites a shift of focus from self to the other. After all, how can you justify looking after yourself when your patients, clients or customers are so needy? Initially, there is a real sense of satisfaction from adding value and improving other people's lives, but, in time, the level of demand feels draining and your sense of self begins to diminish.

The same can happen in fast-moving business environments. The demand to keep improving outputs becomes so linked with progression and self-worth that people believe they have no choice but to put their own needs on hold. Again, for a time it will be exciting and worth the sacrifice, but as time goes by and nothing changes, the demand to put the business first is just too much and the balance breaks down altogether. The end result is an inability to work effectively and delivery suffers.

Action

- If you feel that you are near this point of burnout, arrange some time out of the workplace immediately.
- The urgent need is to return to a balance of focus, so take some time to do things you love – go out into the garden, take walks, read your favourite book, go to the gym … anything that leaves you feeling good about yourself.
- Talk with your manager about support from the Employee

Assistance Programme (EAP), which might have counsellors in your area who you can speak to. If not, speak to your doctor or find a private counsellor and make an appointment.

▶ When you feel up to it, give some thought to your work and whether it is right for you at this time in your life.

▶ If it is, identify what you need in order to maintain a healthy balance of focus.

Excessive focus on yourself

People at the opposite end of the scale who focus primarily on themselves (Figure 5.4) have trouble taking others into account. As a self-focused manager, it is easy to go into tunnel vision and *only* tend to yourself, which is miserable for everyone around you. It leaves your people up in the air, without the information and reinforcement they need. The inevitable output is resentment and people settle for doing a 'good enough' job – after all, if you never notice them, why should they bother?

This happens when personal ambition or the desire to be in control takes over and managers only see the job from one perspective. They take on too much responsibility in the belief that they can do a better job and the team either has to challenge, capitulate or let themselves be sidelined. The manager won't mind being overworked because they have control, but the team perspective is entirely different. Unless they want to be told what to do, it is really hard to work in such a controlling atmosphere. In fact, the boss can end up looking like a bully. Those who are strong enough leave and move on. Others lose their self-esteem and stay put. After all, who else would want them?

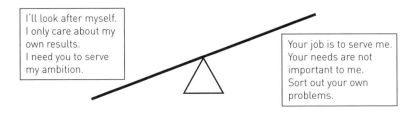

I'll look after myself. I only care about my own results. I need you to serve my ambition.

Your job is to serve me. Your needs are not important to me. Sort out your own problems.

Figure 5.4 Excessive focus on yourself

&& The team ... has to challenge, capitulate or ...
be sidelined. &&

Has this happened to you or do you suspect that this is how people see you? Don't worry, all is not lost. As long as you are keen to learn more and are willing to change, you can still become an inspirational manager.

Action

▶ Think about the last time your team came to you with new ideas. How did you receive them and how open were you to listening? If not, review those ideas now, consider if they are workable and give supportive feedback.

▶ Consider your willingness to seek out other opinions. Choose one thing you need help with and ask the most relevant person what they think. Follow up with an open discussion and look for the right solution, even if it isn't your idea.

▶ 'Go back to the floor' and spend two hours sitting with someone in your team. As you work with them, put yourself in their position and see what you look like, as the boss. How do you imagine you come across? Would you enjoy working with someone like you?

The question of bullying

The perspective of the self-focused manager raises that thorny question of bullying. First of all, what is a bully? There are different definitions and a lot of research that you can access if you need detail. However, in its simplest form, it comes in three main guises.

▶ True bullies enjoy humiliating others. They set out to put people down in order to raise themselves up. They take real delight in seeing people squirm and need constantly to see themselves as better than everyone else. People with these traits should never hold management positions. Their life drivers are totally incompatible with enabling others to do their best work.

▶ Autocrats want their own way. They need to feel in control in order to feel OK and safe. When out of control, they will hit out and blame rather than take responsibility themselves. Autocrats don't set out to put people down, they just need to feel in charge of what is going on around them. They will often accept a challenge when put in the right way, but most people feel too cowed to try.

▶ Self-focused people are unaware of their impact. They have strong, internal ambitions that drive them forward. When they need other people to help them do this, they will be extremely determined and clear about the outputs, timing and style of what they expect. Failure to deliver will bring a strong negative response, resulting from their own frustration. There will be little intention to put others down, just a total lack of concern or awareness of their impact.

For those on the receiving end, the result can feel the same, but the reaction needs to be different. When the behaviour is driven by uncertainty, concern and an inability to handle people well, then it is likely that an appropriate challenge will make a difference. I have worked with a number of apparent 'bullies' who had no idea that this was their impact. Such was their horror when faced with feedback from their people that they have made huge efforts towards change and moved a long way towards positive relationships.

Bullying has become a real minefield and the word can so easily be overused. Of course, it is never acceptable to mistreat another person and such actions must always be dealt with quickly and decisively. However, it is also important not to condone those who cry 'Bully' for the sake of shifting attention away from themselves. The preference for being a 'victim' rather than taking responsibility for inadequate work or poor behaviour makes its own contribution to the problem and can be a form of bullying in its own right.

Managing your own behaviour

Anyone in a position of power must ensure that they never use that power in a way that is negative for other people. So, what do you need to watch for?

As a manager, give some thought to the following.

▶ How do you behave when you feel frustrated and annoyed? How easily will others see this in you? Do you resort to blame or take responsibility for your own mistakes?

▶ How well do you know the people in your team? Are you clear which ones find it difficult when you are cross or frustrated? How vigilant are you about their reactions?

▶ Think back to the last time you lost your temper. Are you clear what the impact was on your team and the people who work around you? Did you take the time to apologise to those who might have been upset or offended? If you're not sure how people were affected, talk with someone in your team who will be honest or ask a peer you know well to give you some feedback

Remember, what you *intend* and what people *receive* might not be the same thing. Make an effort to find out how you are seen and do what you can to bring more balance to the process.

❝ *What you* intend *and what people* receive *might not be the same thing.* ❞

Extreme upward management

Managing upwards in an extreme way is a phenomenon that occurs frequently in business. At first glance it seems to be excessively other-focused, but in fact it is rooted primarily in self-focus. The true desire is to please senior people in order to gain positive feedback and advancement for the self. It is worth understanding because it thrives on ignorance, creating different perceptions of the same person depending where you stand. Leaders see excellence where others see inadequacy and never the two shall meet.

I once coached a manager who was a perfect example of this. Highly valued by the senior leadership, she was given plenty of exciting challenge and loved every minute of it. When the work required her to be primarily self-focused she thrived, but the moment she was given a team problems began to arise. She understood what they had to deliver, but had little idea how to involve and empower them. Like numerous managers before her, she battened down the hatches and did far too much herself. The team struggled to please, doing their best with the instructions provided, but fell far short of the mark.

Within a matter of days, the team was a very unhappy place to work and the manager was thrown into a tailspin, managing the only way she could:

▶ she saw every mistake as threatening her reputation with the senior leadership

71

- so she had to concentrate totally on delivering what the senior leadership wanted
- this ensured they wouldn't see the impact of her management skills
- so she continued to work 24/7 to keep them happy.

Blinded by her sparkling results, they missed the fact that her people were bored, miserable and not delivering well.

There are several repercussions when this happens:

- team members feel undervalued and increasingly resentful
- the manager feels frustrated and misunderstood
- leaders are duped into believing all is well.

The trick is for the manager to refocus and realise that they will achieve more with their teams than on their own. 360-degree feedback can provide an alternative view, but it will only work if people are honest. Alternatively, the managers' manager needs to keep a weather eye by holding skip level meetings with the direct reports so they can explore the other side of the coin.

Managing all your relationships

Of course, you do need to manage upwards. It only becomes a problem when *all* the emphasis goes on managing senior leaders to the exclusion of your direct reports and team because:

- While you make advocates at the senior level of the business, your supporters elsewhere will be few and far between. This will leave you stranded at those times when you need others to deliver work on your behalf.
- Each time you turn away from a peer or direct report to concentrate on the leadership, you reduce the levels of trust around you.
- Your team will feel the pressure of delivering results that make you look good and will resent the fact that you pay them little attention. It becomes unlikely that you will be seen as a great manager to work for, except by those who are equally committed to themselves.

Managing upwards is just one element of their role for inspirational managers. The others are managing sideways and, of course, downwards. As a manager, you need to make sure you have strong and clear relationships all around you, because:

❝ You need to . . . have strong and clear relationships all around you. ❞

▶ Your direct reports are the people who actually do the work. Your job is to manage them and maybe make a tangible contribution to the actual deliverables of the team, depending on the type of work involved. You achieve through them and with them, so the integrity of the relationship will have a profound effect on their outputs.

▶ Your peers support your outputs through their work with their own teams. You need strong and honest relationships so that teams can collaborate effectively together. Peers will also be a prime source of feedback, ideas and a 'listening ear' so you can bounce your ideas around and share experiences of work and people. The degree to which you focus on them and build relationships with them will ensure how supported you feel in your work.

▶ Your senior leaders are also key to the success of your part of the business and, as such, require care and attention. They will determine how well you are kept informed about the business day to day, they know of the opportunities coming up that might be of value to you and your team and they can make your life easy or hard, according to the relationship you have developed.

Can I have balanced focus and still be ambitious?

Without ambition, none of this matters. Work is created through someone having an ambition and others joining in to help them achieve it. Inspirational managers must connect to the ambitions of the business, otherwise it is hard to get excited about the work. However, this doesn't mean that their own ambitions go by the board. Of the managers I met nine months ago, at least four are already in more senior roles. Others are clearly ready for the next opportunity and their managers are on the lookout to ensure that they get it. There is no doubt that when a manager delivers, the business notices and makes the most of that talent. And some also prefer to stay where they are because they know it plays to their strengths and gives them greatest satisfaction and pleasure.

A healthy balance of self and other-focus makes all this much easier because the manager is free to get involved, trusting that they won't be left out in the cold. Instead, they see how much more can be achieved together. The peloton – that vast body of cyclists in the Tour de France – is a perfect example. Each rider in the team has a role to play. Some riders create a safe place and protect the star from other competitors, some go out in front to set the pace and provide a slipstream so that at the right moment the fastest rider can speed out in front and win the race. But they all need the ambition because they actually win the race together.

Much more can be achieved together.

Inspirational managers set such high standards of teamwork that they are the ones most likely to deliver what the business needs, which helps them progress themselves. For example, Tesh Kataria, at Tower Homes, holds the company's vision of providing 'outrageously good service to customers' close to his heart, because it really matters. He trains his team to set a high standard and encourages them at every turn. Everyone has a small musical instrument and every time they move one step closer to putting key workers into their own homes, a cacophony of sound blasts out in celebration. He has made it fun to achieve and the results from the team are far beyond the goals set at the beginning of the year.

Della Garmory, at Nationwide, does the same. A long-time sportswoman and coach and a keen follower of football, she is highly competitive in everything she does and loves to win. Yet, she can still hold that lovely paradox of valuing mistakes for the learning they provide. It is the same need for success that drives her and the team to 'keep going until we get it right'. Giving up is never an option as there is no failure – 'we just didn't get it right this time'. Balanced focus leaves her confident that she and the team will deliver by making appropriate efforts and supporting each other consistently.

Summary

▶ We all need to focus on ourselves *and* others – it is part of being human.

▶ The ideal for an inspirational manager is to create a clear balance between Self-Focus and Other-Focus – this enables you to work well alone *and* with others.

▶ Focusing both on yourself and others will enable you to deliver excellent work in conjunction with other people and ensure that you receive the rewards and accolades for doing so.

▶ It is important to watch for the downside of inbalance:

   – being a pleaser comes from an overload of Other-Focus – it causes confusion, creates frustration in teams and can lead to personal stress and burnout

   – bullying can be an outcome when Self-Focus is high – it may not be intended, but the outcome for those on the receiving end is the same

   – managing upwards is a key behaviour of someone with really strong Self-Focus. It works well for those at the top but can mask problems lower down the company.

▶ Inspirational managers build strong relationships and get satisfaction from the success of others.

▶ Ambition is an important part of the equation – the drive to produce exceptional results is high and they use the strength of relationship to ensure that everyone can do their best work.

Action plan

Today

▶ Work through the questions and identify where your prime area of focus is.

▶ Write down your thoughts about the impact this has on your team, your colleagues and your manager.

▶ Do one thing differently during the day to shift your focus.

Next week

▶ Pay attention to the people in your team. Arrange to go out together for a bit of lunch and just notice how much you are part of the ➤

75

team or if they defer to you. If they do, encourage them to take more responsibility, appreciating them wherever possible.

▶ Notice if the same behaviour occurs in team meetings and, if so, how you feel about it. Are you keen to take centre stage and control the proceedings or do you look for chances to hand over the reins?

▶ Experiment with rotating the chair of the team meeting, so you have to sit back and let others take over.

Next month

▶ Find out if you can get 360-degree feedback and arrange it as soon as possible. Ask for support in debriefing it, preferably from someone expert in this area.

▶ In your one-to-one meetings, ask your people for some feedback. Don't expect it to come easily – it won't be easy for them to criticise the boss. As you show that you are really interested and will act on what they say without repercussions, it will get easier.

▶ Meet with a group of your peers and set up an action learning set (see Appendix 2 for a suggested book on the subject) where you can explore the area of focus together.

▶ Keep a diary of how you spend your time for a week and study it for signs of managing upwards inappropriately. If you find that you are doing this, take a good look at why you feel that you need to and consider what reassurance you are looking for.

CHAPTER

6

The inspirational manager as coach

'Remember, one size won't fit all – be ready to flex your style.'

Daphne De Souza, COI

Many managers use coaching techniques to support their daily work. The main difference is that inspirational managers don't wait for a specific occasion, they use a coaching approach whenever they can. Their natural reaction is to ask open questions with the intention of helping the other person find their own solutions, which is why they are so good at developing talent. Instead of spoon-feeding and instructing, they support people in coming to their own conclusions, which helps them think things through more clearly in the future.

Oliver Hickson, at COI, has trained as a coach and finds that it is a really good way to bring out the best in people. A perfect example was his work with a quiet, unassuming office manager. He discovered that she was so anxious about meeting one of the senior leaders that she kept putting it off: 'To me it made no sense, but the coaching context helped me look at it more constructively and, as we worked through the scenario, she began to gain confidence in her abilities. The result was the first step in a very constructive dialogue, but she could have sat there for six months and not ever had that meeting.'

If Oliver had believed that what you see is what you get, those meetings would never have taken place and a good person would have been lost to the business. This drive to identify talent and use it well provides a real attraction to high performers who will happily trust their development to an inspirational manager. That leads to a virtuous circle – believe in developing talent and talent will find its way to your door, which will enable you and your team to deliver really strong results.

&& *Talent will find its way to your door.* &&

The difference between coaching and mentoring

This is a perennial question on which people have different views. For the purposes of this book, I suggest the following definitions.

▶ *Mentoring* describes a discussion between two people where the emphasis is on the expert sharing their experience to build up the other person's knowledge. The mentor will give opinions freely, describe their experience and give specific advice to the mentee.

▶ *Coaching* describes a discussion between two people where the emphasis is on the coachee learning for themselves. The coach may well have more experience in the subject matter, but will not simply hand out advice. Instead, they will use a coaching approach so the coachee can explore their own understanding and come to their own conclusions.

Periodically in this book I have suggested looking for a mentor who will share learning and experience with you. This is a helpful way of moving beyond your present thinking and will open doors to a new style and understanding. The most productive way to use a mentor is to explore their understanding of a specific issue, think it through for yourself and take on board what is valuable to you. Take care not to merely follow the advice of the mentor since this will limit your development in the long term.

It is also helpful to find a coach who can provide you with a neutral place in which to explore new ideas and their implications. This will be a benefit all round. As Hazel Valentine, at the Academy of Executive Coaching, says, 'When a manager has coaching for themselves, the whole team will benefit from stronger relationships and an increased level of openness.'

Using a coaching style

As an inspirational manager, a coaching style will be the preferred option in many discussions with your people. Using every opportunity to promote personal development, you will always encourage people to think for themselves and not just turn to you for the answers. Stacey Mitchell, at Tower Homes, always begins with a coaching discussion to identify the best way to address problems as they arise. Only if that is not effective will she suggest options to the coachee.

However, there are also specific times to focus on a coaching approach:

- one-to-one meetings
- ad hoc meetings
- delegation.

In all these situations, there is real value to employing a coaching style. Asking questions to help people explore the task at hand in greater depth is the best way for them to learn, develop their strengths and build their understanding of the business. The inspirational manager will ask questions to expand thinking at every opportunity, whether it is just a question in passing or a formal meeting about delegation. Matthew Finlayson, at Data Connection, always coaches Nic Larkin when delegating tasks to him. Matthew can then be sure that Nic is not only doing a great job but also learning as much as he can for his own sake.

Appraisal meetings are totally different. That is a time for you to give feedback and information to your direct report and to hear how they perceive their work to be progressing. It is also an opportunity for you to receive feedback on your management style and discover how else you might help their personal development.

The purpose of coaching

Inspirational managers use coaching for a number of different reasons:

▶ To clarify thinking – providing the opportunity to consider the implications of an action

▶ To explore new ideas – encouraging innovative thinking and big picture awareness

▶ To come to decisions and understand the consequences of those decisions.

Day-to-day business is very demanding. E-mails dominate, phone calls distract and people ask advice and questions, so the time to stop and think about the implications of a piece of work is hard to find, not to mention the challenges of a new venture or some personal development. So, for your direct reports to know that you will take time to help them understand the different elements of their work is a big positive for them.

For most people, meetings with managers are fast, output-focused and time-limited. Think about the last meeting you had with your own manager. My guess is that you had a long list of things you wanted to talk about, were probably up against a deadline and mobiles were buzzing like demented bees, alerting you both 'silently'! Not much room for thought there, then!

❝ Time to think more deeply ... is a real gift. ❞

Instead, suppose your manager had been in full listening mode, keen to understand and explore your thoughts and concerns on the subject in question. This would make it so much easier for you to think through that new piece of work, the ideas you have come up with to improve the effectiveness of your team or your concerns about how to handle a difficult people problem you are facing. Time to think more deeply with a familiar person to help you focus your thoughts is a real gift in this fast-moving world of work.

The range of conversations

When Bob Henry was CEO of CORGI, he used to sit in an open space where people could speak to him at any time. To make sure that he was responding at the right level, he would always begin by asking, 'What sort of conversation do you want?' By being direct, he could ensure he responded at the right level.

Getting clear in your mind the difference between styles of conversations will help you respond flexibly to the needs of your people. The main discussions at work will be:

▶ social conversations

▶ management input and discussions

▶ coaching support.

All are supportive conversations that help others move forward in their work, but in each one the definition of support varies to accommodate the differences in power and relationship. Once you understand these subtle differences, you will feel more comfortable in a coaching role.

❝Supportive conversations . . . help others move forward in their work. ❞

Having a social chat

In chats with friends, you define support as them feeling valued, good about themselves and good about you. This means that you:

▶ listen to what they say with the intention of supporting them

▶ accept their view of the world and go along with it

▶ share stories of your own experience and what happened

▶ tell them what you think they should do, but back off if they don't agree

▶ tell little white lies rather than upset them.

Essentially, you are joining the other person's worldview and helping them to justify it. Your job is not to open up thinking but support their polemic, and if that means putting aside your own power for a short time, you may well do it for the sake of your friend. You will have done your job if your friend feels calm and good about themselves.

A management conversation

Support in a management capacity demands that you provide the right information in a timely manner so that the person can deliver results in a way that leaves them feeling positive about themselves. This means that you:

▶ listen to what they say so that you can make sure they are going in the right direction

▶ tell them your view of the world, so that they understand what they need to do

▶ tell them what is going on in the business so that they have the full picture

▶ give them instructions about what they need to focus on

▶ tell them clearly when they are on the wrong lines.

You have the understanding and big picture view that the other is lacking and sharing it will enable them to move forward in the direction you want. You hold power, so other people join you in your worldview and may not speak out because of it.

A coaching conversation

In a coaching conversation, support means helping the coachee have a clear view of the implications of their action so that they can make effective choices and deliver the required outputs. This requires you to:

▶ listen to what is said so you have a good understanding of the situation

▶ accept their worldview, but also look at the impact they have on those with a different worldview

▶ share your experience *only* if it is highly relevant and will build their understanding

▶ encourage them to look at the situation from different perspectives so that they can make informed decisions

▶ challenge their thinking so they understand their impact and can learn from what is happening around them.

As a coach, you sit outside any specific worldview in order to help them see more clearly. You challenge them to step outside their own polemic, so that they can make informed decisions. You will be doing a good job if your coachee feels challenged, a bit discomforted with plenty to think about and has a 360-degree view of the situation.

❝ You will be doing a good job if your coachee feels challenged, a bit discomforted with plenty to think about and has a 360-degree view. ❞

What this tells us

All three conversations are about power and focus. According to the situation, you take on the power or give it up for others. The coaching context requires that you put aside your power in order to help people understand and make their own choices.

Coaching interventions

Getting to grips with the complexities of coaching will take more than reading this chapter, so find out if your organisation can offer you a course internally or book you a place on one designed specifically for managers. This said, there are a few basic interventions that will start you off and enable you to experiment with coaching your team on specific issues.

Remember, your aim is to encourage the other person to explore their own thinking rather than just tell them what to do, so you need the questions and comments that will open their minds to other options. You will achieve this through:

▶ active listening

▶ offering supportive comments

▶ providing creative ideas.

❝Your aim is to encourage the other person to explore their own thinking.❞

Active listening

This is the most important element of your coaching toolkit and the best gift you can offer to your coachees. It is extremely rare to have someone truly listen, so never underestimate the impact you will have by doing just that! Most people listen for a gap so that they can add in their own experience or tell the person what to do. Active listening, on the other hand, takes in all the elements of what is being said and explores them fully.

There are three elements to active listening.

▶ *Reflecting back* – Take the words the person has just used and repeat them back – that is, 'you feel exhausted, trying to get the project up and running'. It feels odd to do this initially, but it can be very useful for the coachee to hear exactly what they have said. It helps them clarify whether this is really how they feel or it is just one aspect of the issue.

▶ *Questioning to understand* – In coaching it is important not to make assumptions, so repeat what you have understood and ask if that is right. For example, 'So you are saying that you felt ignored when the person spoke that way – is that right?' This has a three-fold purpose:

 – you can make sure that you truly understand what is being said and give your coachee the opportunity to provide you with a fuller picture

 – it enables the person to explore their own thinking further as they hear another person's reaction

 – it makes it very clear that you are listening fully and are interested in what they are saying, which contributes to trust building.

▶ *Summarising* – This is another technique that enables the coachee to consider the subject matter. Your task as the coach is to pause periodically to summarise the discussion so far. It is a form of reflection but brings the whole piece together and it will be helpful for the coachee to hear the links you make between the different elements of the situation.

This is called active listening because you don't just listen quietly, you use what you have heard to help the speaker to clarify, explore and understand more fully what they are saying. The impact of hearing someone else speak your own words is remarkable. It makes them very real, provides another level of meaning and makes very clear that you are not alone with your issue.

Active listening also demonstrates why it is so important for inspirational managers to focus fully on other people. If you are primarily self-focused (see Chapter 5) you can't provide the quality of listening required for an effective coaching session. In active listening you are paying attention to the nuances of what is being said, taking heed of every element of the conversation and linking from one part of the discussion to another. There is no room for thinking about how you are coming across or what you want to say because you are totally other-focused.

Offering supportive comments

It can be really useful to offer supportive comments with a desire to help and move forward. These include.

- ▶ Comments and body language that show you are listening. These are little gestures that you probably do anyway when taking in what someone is telling you:
  - – nodding your head
  - – comments that demonstrate you are tracking the conversations, such as, 'I see', 'Mmm'.

- ▶ Acknowledgement of the impact of a situation, such as, 'I imagine that must have felt really exciting', 'I get the impression you were longing to speak out'.

- ▶ Bringing in a little humour. When appropriate, this can lighten the atmosphere in a helpful way – 'I have a picture of you bouncing off the walls of the office!', for example. This can also help the coachee gain a perspective on events rather than drown in their own concerns.

- ▶ Validation of their experiences and reactions, such as, 'It sounds to me as if your actions have had a positive effect on the situation', 'I think that I might have kept quiet at that point, too'.

▶ Sharing personal experiences. This can be useful as long as it is totally relevant and you mention it with the intention of helping the other person move forward. To hear that they are not alone in struggling with a situation is really useful and can take away some of the pressure. 'I can really understand that feeling of being overwhelmed by work', for example.

To make it clear when something is just your opinion, begin sentences with:

▶ 'I imagine ... '

▶ 'I notice ... '

▶ 'I'm curious about ... '

▶ 'I think ... '

▶ 'It sounds to me as if ... '

The main question to ask yourself is 'Why do I want to make a supportive comment?' Is it because you truly feel that it will help the other person expand their understanding or because you want to steer the conversation in a particular direction? If it is the former, then go for it; if it is the latter, then put the thought on one side for later.

Providing creative ideas

You may well have some really good ideas during a coaching conversation and it is important to add them in if you feel they will be of value. Again, your first question needs to be, 'Am I offering up the idea for the benefit of the other or because I want to influence their behaviour?'

▶ If ideas come to you during the discussion, make a quick note so you don't forget them.

▶ Consider whether the idea is relevant in this setting or not. Will it really take the person forward in a positive way?

▶ If you decide that there is real value, give two or three additional ideas for the coachee to consider, so that there is no risk they take your one idea as an instruction.

▶ If the coachee doesn't pick it up, don't force it on them – this is their discussion not yours.

▶ If you still believe that the idea is of value, find a way to use it yourself.

The main challenge is to give up your attachment to being right. The only 'right' in this discussion is what is appropriate for the coachees.

Stages in a coaching session

There will be times when it is appropriate to sit down with one of your people for a coaching session to concentrate on a specific learning need or work issue. Using specific coaching techniques and methodology will maximise learning and model how to think through issues in the future.

While the coachee will dictate the content of the conversation, your job as coach is to manage the process carefully to ensure that all the following stages are covered in the time frame.

1 prepare for the coaching conversation

2 set the agenda

3 explore the subject

4 discuss the options

5 come to a conclusion and set an action plan.

1 Prepare for the coaching conversation

You may need a moment of personal time to reorientate yourself to a coaching style, especially if you have been working on your own or contributing to a business meeting. You need to make the shift to focusing on the other person, so giving some thought to your own needs first will enable you to then turn fully to the other.

Once you are ready for the session, begin by setting some clear parameters for the discussion.

Action

▶ Find a quiet location where you will be undisturbed for the duration of the discussion.

▶ Agree that this is a coaching discussion so the person knows what to expect. Doing this formally also helps to shift the power dynamic from a manager–direct report to coach–coachee relationship.

▶ Agree a clear time frame together so you can relax and not worry about other work demands.

2 Set the agenda

Once you know that the person needs to explore an issue, ask them to tell you exactly what it is they need. Never assume that you know already or attempt to use this time for your own agenda. If you need specific outputs from the person, set a time for that specific discussion rather than attempt to hijack coaching time.

Sometimes your coachee will have a very clear idea of what they want from the discussion, so can tell you exactly the line they want to explore. Other times, they may have a general theme and need you to help them pin down which is the most important aspect to explore. If so, then this is the first step in your coaching process and may even be the subject matter itself.

Action

▶ Ask the person to outline the subject matter they want to explore.

▶ Find out why it is important – this will spell out the external factors involved.

▶ Be as specific as possible about what they need to clarify, decide and act on as a result of the coaching.

▶ Find out what a 'good' result will look like by the end of the discussion.

▶ Make notes of the agenda to help you stay on track.

3 Explore the subject

The third stage in coaching is to explore fully the issue at hand. As obvious as this sounds, it is something that happens rarely in day-to-day conversation. Think back to the last time you talked to a colleague about a difficulty you were facing. Did they listen well and ask you to elaborate on your thoughts about it? Probably not. It is much more likely that your colleague listened until they got the gist of the problem, then gave you their opinion or advice!

Learning about other people and understanding their perspective is a fundamental driver for an inspirational manager. Not only do they really want to understand, but also realise that it will help them manage others in the future – up, down and sideways. It is also a matter of truly empowering someone to find their own way, so Charlotte Butterfield, at Badenoch & Clark, speaks of 'planting seeds so people can come up with their own ideas in future'.

❝ Keep your questions as open as possible. ❞

Aim to keep your questions as open as possible so that the coachee is encouraged to get to grips with what the issue is really about. So, use comments or questions like:

- ▶ Talk me through your thinking and how you came to this conclusion.
- ▶ What was happening when you first realised you had a problem?
- ▶ What options have you identified so far?
- ▶ Tell me more about that.
- ▶ Put yourself in the other person's shoes and tell me about the situation.

At regular intervals, check that you have understood correctly by reflecting back or summarising what you have heard. 'So you are saying ... Have I got that right?' This gives the speaker the chance to correct any misconceptions and, in telling you more clearly, there is also a good chance that they will understand more about the issue themselves.

Exploring the true issue

I once coached a manager on dealing with a performance issue in his team. When we set the agenda, his main concern was just how bad the person was at the job, despite the fact that he regularly pointed out mistakes and told them where they had gone wrong. It would have been very easy to look for ways to handle such a difficult employee, but I wasn't convinced that we had got to the root of the issue. It is rare for a situation to be this clear-cut, so we explored different elements of the relationship, only to find that the team had had a very rocky year, with this person joining at the most difficult time.

I suggested that the manager put himself in the other person's shoes and, suddenly, the penny dropped. He was spending so much time shouting about what was wrong that he had forgotten to mention when it was right. His direct report was losing heart and couldn't be bothered to make the effort – he no longer believed that he could win.

Hard as it was, the manager had to take on board that his report was suffering from his own lack of good will. Being so wrapped up in his negative belief, he was exacerbating the problem. This action was to spend time understanding life through the eyes of his direct report, making a point of looking for what was right. It gave him a positive outcome and took away the need to address underperformance altogether.

Action

▶ Enter into each coaching discussion with curiosity. It will be very interesting to explore what it driving the issue.

▶ Begin with the assumption that there is more to it than meets the eye. This isn't about a lack of trust it just acknowledges that if it was straightforward, you wouldn't need this conversation.

▶ Listen to what is said and reflect back what you have heard. This will give the person a chance to clarify and expand what they have told you so far.

▶ If the person shows sign of emotion, give them space and encourage them to talk it through. Be sympathetic and show that you accept where they are. If you suspect there is more, ask the coachee to talk about the reason for them being upset, angry or frustrated.

▶ At the end of this part of the discussion, summarise what you think is the issue to be addressed and find out if they agree.

4 Discuss the options

Once you have a clear idea of what the issue actually is, then it is much easier to look for the options.

A word of warning. If you find the coachee looking for reasons why they can't follow up apparently good options, you have probably moved to this stage too soon. You may well be looking for answers to the wrong problem or have not fully expanded the complexities of the issue, in which case move back into the exploration stage until you are both clear.

Action

▶ Ask the coachee to describe the issue and the questions that need to be answered, as these may now be different from the original presenting issue. For example, the manager in the example above needed to find options for building a relationship rather than dismissing the employee.

▶ Once you are both clear about the issue, ask the coachee to talk through the options that come to mind.

▶ Help them to consider all aspects of the options they present by asking the coachee to talk through the pros and cons. If you can see consequences that they haven't thought of, frame a question that will encourage the coachee to think it through more. Resist the temptation just to tell.

▶ If you have ideas, feel free to add them on to the list. Make it clear that you are not attached to them picking up the suggestion unless it feels right and be watchful for someone doing so just because you said it.

---

5 Come to a conclusion and set an action plan

It is really important to finish a coaching session with a commitment to action, so make sure that you leave enough time for this stage of the process. One of the benefits of coaching is that it supports people to take new actions or change their behaviour, but this will be hard to do if the outcomes are vague or unmanageable, so make sure you pin down the next steps together.

" *Finish a coaching session with a commitment to action.* "

A great way to do this is by making the actions SMART – that is:

- ▶ Specific
- ▶ Measurable
- ▶ Achievable
- ▶ Realistic
- ▶ Time limited.

Going through this process will make sure that the actions are really manageable and valuable to the work situation.

Action

- ▶ Ask your coachee to identify the option that they think is most relevant and that they can fully commit to.
- ▶ Talk through the actions they need to take to move the ideas forward.
- ▶ Create a plan together that is specific and time bound.
- ▶ Ask questions if you think that the time frames won't work or the specific elements of the action are not manageable.
- ▶ Explore the coachee's picture of success and make sure that you think it is possible – if not, ask questions that will help them to be more realistic.
- ▶ Make a note of it yourself and read back what you have heard and understood, just to make sure that you are both in agreement.
- ▶ Agree a time to meet and talk through the results so the coachee can take the learning from their experience.

Giving advice

There will be times when you are dying to get in there and give advice. In fact, that is *not* your job as a coach. Remember, the focus is on the other person and their learning, so if you wade in with your thoughts, you stop their development. However, there are a few occasions when it may be of value to share your opinion.

The temptation is most likely to arise in two ways:

- when the coachee asks for your advice
- when you are concerned about the ideas the coachee is coming up with.

When the coachee asks for your advice

A less confident coachee will want to be told what to do and it may be relevant to share your opinion, given your wider experience of the organisation and business. Coaching doesn't mean that you never do this, but it does mean you have to be very careful to do it in a way that provides options and encourages people to think for themselves.

You can keep the learning element by pacing when you give your view:

- make it clear that you want to know what they think first, but then you will be happy to offer them your thoughts
- ask them to talk through their concerns, ideas and thoughts about the issue
- ask questions to explore what they are saying, so they discover benefits and drawbacks to ideas or actions
- suggest that they put themselves in your shoes and see what the answers might look like
- ask, 'If you already knew the answer, who would it look like/sound like' – remarkable as it sounds, people often answer this really well!

Once they have really thought through the pros and cons for themselves, then let them know what you think and why. Ensure that final decisions remain with them, making it clear that this is your view and not a definitive answer.

When you are concerned about the ideas the coachee is coming up with

If you are really concerned about the ideas that are emerging, you need to take some form of action, but, again, in a way that doesn't take the power away from the coachee.

▶ Identify the piece that you are concerned about. For example, 'I am interested in your idea to ... let's explore that for a moment.'

▶ Ask them to talk you through the pros and cons, so that they have to look at all the implications of their ideas.

▶ Keep an open mind at this stage – it may be that they have a perspective that you haven't taken fully into account.

▶ If you are still concerned and believe an important piece is being missed, then put your concern into a question for them: 'What do you think will happen if ... ?'

▶ If you do have to speak directly, then do it in a way that won't put the other person down: 'If I was on the receiving end, I think I would respond in this way, so let's see if that impacts on your plan.'

It is important to recognise that you won't always be right and, even if you are, creative mistakes can be useful. So, choose the moments when you speak out. You don't want harm to come to the person or the business, but they may need to make some of their own mistakes.

❝ Creative mistakes can be useful. ❞

Robert Hiscox, chairman of Hiscox Insurance, has been in the business for so long that there are few new ideas for him to hear. Yet, he realises that to keep saying, 'We tried that and it didn't work' will deaden creativity. He also believes that the idea may just work this time or at least that the person will learn a lot from the mistake. As a result, he only speaks out if he sees a real risk from pursuing an activity.

Summary

▶ Inspirational managers take every opportunity to coach so that their people understand how to learn and expand their thinking.

▶ *Mentors* provide you with information, *coaches* encourage you to find your own answers.

▶ Styles of conversation vary according to the required outcome. It is important to identify the requirements of each discussion as it arises. ▶

- Active listening is an important coaching technique that is valuable in many situations. Offering supportive comments and creative ideas are also useful tools in a coaching conversation.

- Sometimes you need to hold a specific coaching session. This has a number of stages:

  1 preparing for the coaching conversation

  2 set the agenda

  3 explore the subject

  4 discuss the options

  5 come to a conclusion and set an action plan.

- It is not the job of a coach to give advice. Where it will be useful to share your ideas, make sure that you do it in a way that maintains the coachees' ability to choose for themselves.

Action plan

Today

- Find out about the coaching courses on offer to you.

- Use one of the elements of active listening in your next conversation to give you a practice run.

Next week

- Identify a direct report who would benefit from a coaching session. Linking this to some delegated work would be ideal.

- Set a time in the diary for a coaching session.

- Set aside some time to plan how you will manage the session and make some notes on what you need to pay attention to.

- Practise active listening in all your conversations, whether coaching or not.

Next month

- Look for a coaching opportunity each week and use the skills you have practised.

- At the end of each discussion, ask for some feedback and use it to improve your approach.

> ▶ Find yourself a coach in the organisation or externally so that you can experience it from the other side – this will be really helpful.
>
> ▶ Book yourself on to a programme of some form to improve your skills.

CHAPTER 7

Building inspirational teams

'Never stop asking questions and never feel like you are on your own – just keep encouraging teamwork and consultation.'

Andrew Rothesay, Boehringer Ingelheim

'At Tower Homes, we're like a family. Sometimes it's all really nice and sometimes it's extremely demanding – just like any other family.' In fact, as Stacey Mitchell points out, 'You may think it's a soft touch, but when people know each other this well the pressure to perform is extremely high. If friendship isn't involved, there is less to lose.' When you care about someone, you really don't want to let them down, which is great for standards and the business.

❝ When you care about someone, you really don't want to let them down. ❞

Inspirational managers build fantastic teams that top-quality people fall over themselves to get into because they know these managers will make the most of their careers. We are talking:

- ▶ high trust
- ▶ challenging work
- ▶ good fun
- ▶ plenty of support.

They congratulate, celebrate and struggle alongside their people, delivering the targets and learning from mistakes along the way. Who wouldn't want to work in that environment?

Think about your own team for a moment.

- ▶ Is that the sort of atmosphere you have?
- ▶ Are really good people lining up to work with you?
- ▶ What reputation do you have as a team manager?

Highly productive teams contain skilled people who are excellent at their jobs, proud to work with their colleagues and really want the team and organisation to succeed. They will all be different. Some will be full of laughter and chat, others will be much quieter, but all will suit the task and the people involved and all are great places to work for the team members.

So, how do you go about creating a high-performing, inspirational team for your people to work in? The underpinning element is your personal development as an inspirational manager, which is addressed throughout this book. When you really inspire your team, they will deliver great results and aspire to be the very best. However, you also have to address any obstacles in the system or the team functioning, so they don't waste time dealing with extraneous happenings.

❝ When you really inspire your team, they will deliver great results. ❞

The team's framework

The first step in achieving an inspirational team environment is to build a strong framework that ensures positive relationships are maintained through good *and* tough times. Regardless of your area of work, this will help the team thrive and 'sing its own song'.

1 Dream the ideal team for your work.

2 Set the team charter.

3 Build the team.

4 Agree communication styles.

❝ Build a strong framework that ensures positive relationships are maintained. ❞

1 Dream the ideal team for your work

Whether you are starting a new team or continuing to work with the same team, it is always worth taking some quiet time to dream about your ideal and what it will look like in your part of the business.

Action

▶ Think about the sort of team you need to deliver the agreed outcomes.

▶ Compare this to your ideal team to work in and see how they might come together.

▶ Look at it from the point of view of your people and see what they need in order to enjoy their work and do a great job.

▶ Let the dream clarify in your mind and imagine what it would be like to work in that team on a daily basis.

Make some notes about the main features – these sorts of dream thoughts are very easily lost in the heat of the day job.

2 Set the team charter

You can't build a team on your own, so your next challenge is to get your people interested in the prospect of working in a different way. You can do this by sharing your dream, building it to the next stage with them and deciding exactly what life needs to look like in the future.

Once you are all in agreement on the vision, developing a team charter is a fantastic way to both unite people behind the dream and get specific about what it means. You need to agree the behaviour that each person must adopt if you are to deliver the dream. This serves a three-fold purpose:

▶ it provides a clear framework for everyone to follow

▶ it enables you to spot when someone is losing heart and needs support

▶ it provides a context for a tough conversation when someone is not following the agreed behaviour.

Action

▶ Arrange for a team meeting away from telephones and e-mail. Allow a good chunk of time for it – two hours at least.

▶ Talk the team through your dream, how you visualise the team working together and the impact this will have on their work. Be as enthusiastic as you like so that your people feel inspired to join you!

➤

> ▶ Go into listening mode and ask for comments – what they like, don't like and any other ideas they have. The output from this discussion needs to be a dream that everyone can get excited about.

> ▶ Talk about the behaviours you all need to adopt if you are to make the dream a reality and make a clear agreement that everyone can buy into. By the end of this discussion, everyone should understand how to behave with their colleagues from now on – this is your team charter.

> ▶ Make it clear that you will build this behaviour into your one-to-one meetings and appraisals. This will show how serious you are about making this a fantastic team.

'I'm important and I want to be respected'

This statement from an induction trainer on Tesh Kataria's first ever day at work stays with him still. It seemed a bit arrogant at the time – you can imagine! However, he went on to say, 'If you learn nothing else today, remember *everyone* has that voice in their head, so they all deserve your respect.'

Hardly surprising then, that Tesh, at Tower Homes, has a strong team who work extremely well together. Their job is to house key workers – nurses, police, teachers – in expensive South London. There are nine set steps between an application and getting the door keys. In order to improve job variety and ensure that they all know what their colleagues are doing, Tesh moves the team members around at regular intervals. Sometimes they work alone, sometimes in pairs and sometimes each member of the team has one step in the process. In team meetings, they talk together about how to restructure. When I met them they were taking each task on a weekly rota – an idea that came from the team that was going well.

Tesh wants people to take as much responsibility as possible, even to the point of tending to the smooth running of the team. Early on in an interview, he will ask how they would handle someone who wasn't pulling their weight. He doesn't want people who just hand everything over to him. Instead, they need to find out what's happening and look for the solution, which may involve speaking to him about it but it may be something that they can act on independently.

The level of individual involvement is high, including in the weekly team meeting. ➤

▶ It has an agenda with a clear start and finish time.

▶ They share 'Well done's and 'Thank you's within the team.

▶ They talk about 'Moans and groans', but always with solutions.

Recent discussions included a concern that too many customers were being put through to voicemail. No one liked this – it doesn't fit with the team ethos – so now the telephone system has been changed so it searches for someone who is free. They also suggested and implemented a team phone number that any member of the team can answer.

Another important issue was the making of tea and coffee. Tesh believes that small issues like this can turn into bigger problems if not attended to. The original pattern was that anyone who wanted a drink offered to make other people one while they were there. That worked OK until the arrival of a prolific tea drinker, who was soon losing time tending to the rehydration of the team! So together they created a daily rota that ensures each team member makes the drinks just once a week, but guarantees each person two drinks a day – any more than that and they make it themselves. Tesh is, of course, included and enjoys his rota days for the chance it gives him to have a bit of fun with the rest of the team!

3 Build the team

Don't just think about a one-off fun day, but a constant process. Inspirational teams are built on strong relationships, which require shared experiences and fun. You don't need to spend a fortune – talking through the team's challenges in an inclusive way and involving everyone in celebrating each success is a great start.

❝Inspirational teams . . . require shared experiences and fun.❞

Some teams are made up of people who would never be friends, but this won't stop them working well together. It is a fascinating challenge to find the common ground between people with different personalities, ethnicity, ages, genders and preferences. You will get there as long as you set a tone of open exploration – the process of finding out about each other is the perfect start to great teamwork. Human beings are inherently curious, so looking for what links us is a rewarding task, as long as we set about it with respect and genuine interest in the other.

" Set a tone of open exploration. "

The key to any teamwork is openness, so make sure that your charter includes something about being honest. For example:

- ▶ if you feel confused, ask
- ▶ if you get it wrong, say sorry and look for the learning
- ▶ if you need to understand more, have a conversation.

There are many different ways in which to build a team. Helena Moore, at Bromford Housing Group, is a great believer in little and often. Every manager at Bromford has a budget for teambuilding and celebration, but they found that most weren't using it. They started an initiative – 'give up being Victor Meldrew and be Mrs Doyle – go on, go on, go on, use your allowance'. Helena uses some of her money to provide a welcome to the wider team. Whenever a new person arrives, she ties a helium balloon to the water fountain. This alerts everyone in the building to the presence of another balloon somewhere in the office: 'You'll find it tied to the desk of the newcomer, so go and say "Hello" and have a chocolate.'

Paul Dunmore, at Thomson Directories, uses competition to bring the team together. 'I badgered the boss to set up a team competition to give us something to work for. We've been the top-performing team for four out of the last five years. The prize is a lump sum for us to do something we can enjoy together and we've been to Dublin, Milan and Florence. We take partners – they deserve it after getting earache all year when we come in late and cheesed off. Once I know the budget, I sit on the Internet and find out where the cheap flights are going. First we went to Dublin because it was "local", then I realised you could get cheap flights to all sorts of places.'

Action

- ▶ Look at the present work challenges and consider how you can use them to bring the team together. You could have lunch or a coffee together to explore the situation and options.

- ▶ Ask one person each week to start off the team meeting by introducing something new about themselves.

- ▶ Talk with other managers and see if you can create some form of competition or collaboration that will focus attention on outputs. This will not only build your team but also create links across the bigger organisational team.

- ▶ If in doubt about the best way to progress, talk to the team and use it as a teambuilding discussion in its own right.

Agendas for teambuilding

The two best agendas for teambuilding are:

- ▶ team development via business goals
- ▶ team development via personal learning.

Team development via business goals

Formal teambuilding sessions work best when linked directly to the business, otherwise there is a risk that people won't see the point. Andrew Rothesay, at Boehringer Ingelheim, wanted to engage his remote team in the new vision of being world class, so he set up an overnight meeting and took them to Le Manoir Aux Quat' Saisons, a top-class, Michelin-starred restaurant and hotel in Oxfordshire. They had an excellent working lunch and Raymond Blanc came in to talk about how he made his vision a reality, what keeps him going and the values he holds. He was really inspiring and with people asking him questions, it was a stimulating and exciting session. Andrew then split the team up and sent them out to enjoy the fabulous venue. It set them all talking and gave them time to wonder what it was all about.

Next day, they explored what it means to be world class, using their experience of Le Manoir as a starting point. The output was a detailed vision that they could roll out throughout the wider sales team. Andrew was pleased with the result: 'There was loads of energy and they were fired up to really get into our own version of excellence. While it was a big investment, it enabled us to go out and successfully engage and fire up 80 per cent of our 50-strong sales management group, a business return that far outweighs the financial investment.'

It doesn't have to cost a fortune, it just needs to link to the business or team concept. Andrew didn't see how he could exhort them to function at an elite level without demonstrating that they were worth that standard of service themselves. On the basis that we give what we receive, he wanted them to have a direct experience of what he was talking about.

Action

▶ Consider the organisation's vision and strategy for the next year. What will this demand of your team?

▶ Look for ways to help your people get a feel for what this will mean. Vision is all about emotion, so doing something that links to feelings will be highly effective.

▶ If you have a budget for your team, be Mrs Doyle – go on, go on ... use it! If you don't have a budget, put together a proposal for a team celebration and take it to your manager for action.

▶ If you are struggling to think of ideas, link with a couple of managers from related teams and explore how you can collaborate on some form of event or meeting.

▶ Bring team members together to look at the year ahead and work out what it means for them. Make sure you come out of the time with clear, agreed actions and agreements.

Team development via personal learning

Personal development is another great forum for teambuilding, especially as it is so fundamental to the style of an inspirational manager. It improves the levels of support once everyone understands the challenges their colleagues are facing and provides an opportunity to share experiences. Getting them talking together about strengths and weaknesses means that:

▶ they get immediate feedback on their impact from people who know them well

- everyone learns about coaching and real listening
- ideas are shared and suggestions made for positive change
- the level of contact in the team is greatly improved.

If this would be new behaviour for the team, get help from a good facilitator to start you off and ensure that you have high-quality conversations.

❝Bring your people together in a way that they will enjoy. ❞

Whether it is Raymond Blanc, a weekend in Dublin or an evening at the local pub is irrelevant, as long as it fits the team and the business, go for it. The important thing is to bring your people together in a way that they will enjoy, to start them talking in a different way and to give them an experience of what life can be like in a really outstanding team.

Action

- Use your one-to-one discussions to review strengths and development areas.
- If your work will allow you to bring people together for a chunk of time, get each person to talk about the strengths others can call on and where they need help from others.
- If your work demands that meetings are kept short, have a quick five minutes in your next team meeting for a bit of 'speed dating' – in pairs, each person has to say one thing that they appreciate about the other and one thing they would like them to change.
- Follow up on their learning in your subsequent one-to-ones.

---

4 Agree communication styles

Inspirational managers are always concerned to stay informed, involve everyone and make sure the team have the information they need. There are two aspects to this:

- your communication to the team – you need to keep your team informed of business changes and progress
- the team's communication to you – they need to keep you informed about their work, any personal concerns and ideas for improvements.

109

Your communication to the team

You are the team's direct link to other parts of the business, so make sure that you have an effective way of keeping them up to date. It is relatively easy to set up meetings that provide information, so all you have to do then is make sure they happen.

Della Garmory, from Nationwide, lives a long way from work so uses her travel time to speak to her team. Monday morning is the special time when she leaves them all a collective voicemail to start the week. It has a number of components.

- ▶ 'Hope you had a nice weekend.'
- ▶ Something about what she did herself, a bit of fun.
- ▶ Information about her diary for the week.
- ▶ The opportunity to add anything they need her to do.
- ▶ Ending with 'have a great week'.

It is something they all look forward to and it starts the week off really well.

It doesn't matter how you do it, just find the way that suits you and do it consistently. Oliver Hickson, from COI, was given feedback a couple of years ago that he didn't communicate enough, so now he lets his team members know everything. He was worried at first that he had gone too far, but he has been reassured that he has got it just right.

- ▶ He uses a combination of e-mails and face-to-face time
- ▶ He makes a point of keeping the gap between him knowing and them knowing as short as possible
- ▶ He stays on top of the rumour mill – there is one person in his team who is really easy to talk to and acts a bit like the 'mother' of the team, so he makes sure she keeps him up to date with the gossip.

The team's communication to you

It must be just really easy for the team to reach you, so make sure you are known to be approachable – it is your best insurance against disaster. Please beware of being complacent and thinking, 'Well, I do have an open door policy', so do some of the *least* approachable managers I have ever met! For people to feel easy about speaking to you, you need:

- open relationships
- to understand your people
- a reputation for listening well
- no blame.

Only then will your open door be of value!

Be approachable – it is your best insurance against disaster.

Nic, at Data Connection, has weekly communication meetings to talk through the status of the work his team is doing, but he also emphasises the importance of spot discussions throughout the week. He drums into people, 'If it's not going right, talk to me or someone else in the team. Don't hold on to concerns.'

Action

- When did you last sit down with your team members to tell them what is happening in the business? Are they up to date right now? If not, set regular update meetings in your diary for the next six months and stick to them.

- At your next team meeting, find out if people are getting enough information. If not, ask what they want to know about and either tell them or find out in time for the next meeting.

- Remember back to when someone last came to you with a concern or idea. If it was a long time, then think about how approachable you are. Get feedback from team members on what they need in order to speak more easily with you.

Managing adversity

Being a team manager means giving support when people need it, unconditionally. Sue Mooney, at Nationwide, knows first hand the value of this. She also knows how it impacts on her commitment to the organisation in the future.

111

I started to work with Della just before I become pregnant and I wouldn't have got through it without her help. It wasn't an easy pregnancy, but Della did everything she could to make my life easier – like reducing the amount of travel I had to do and reserving an easy parking space for me every day. Things like that really helped.

I came back after four months, but pretty soon realised I wasn't well – in fact, I had postnatal depression. I carried on as long as I could, but one day I just felt completely overwhelmed and couldn't turn in for work. Della was completely supportive from day one ... she never once made me feel guilty at leaving the team with my workload and taking the time I needed to recover.

I was entitled to a number of counselling sessions through the Nationwide health scheme, which was a considerable help, just not long enough. Della stepped in and offered to cover the costs so that I could continue with the additional treatment until I was well. She provided just the right level of support – I was able to speak or meet with her whenever I needed to.

I'm pleased to say I've been back at work for some time now and going from strength to strength. It wasn't easy, but Della managed my return with sensitivity. I slowly took on more and more work, gradually increased my hours; eventually moving from a 'condensed' four-day week to my current full-time hours.

I had never experienced a manager being as supportive and understanding as Della was during my illness and I often wonder if I'd still be working at Nationwide now had she not been my manager then.

Developing your own team style

Charlotte Butterfield, from Badenoch & Clark, hates the phrase, 'if it ain't broke don't fix it'. 'It is absolutely ridiculous! You've got to be tweaking all the time – you've got to be passionate about improving your teams. I want each of my teams to be the best in the company.'

Your task as an inspirational manager is to create an exciting and dynamic workplace where people love coming in each day and are keen to do a really good job. Because we are all human, that means a place where they can:

▶ have a laugh every now and then

▶ feel confident to speak out when they have made a mess

▶ challenge your thinking with a better idea and feel valued for it.

❝ Create an exciting and dynamic workplace where people love coming in each day and are keen to do a really good job. ❞

So, your job is to find the way of working that suits everyone and will allow you both to support them and get out of the way once they know what they are doing.

There is no right way to do this – just your way – but there are some common themes that all inspirational managers need to consider, so that they can work out the way that suits them and their teams best.

▶ Can I have people in the team who are better than me?

▶ Can a manager be friends with direct reports?

▶ Is open plan or a separate office best?

▶ Is my place inside or outside of the team?

All these questions beset every manager with a team to lead. Just what is the best way to go about it?

Can I have people in the team who are better than me?

An inspirational manager will always answer with a resounding 'Yes!' Never mind if direct reports know more than you – after all, your job is to build an inspirational team and manage proceedings, not do all the work yourself.

Ian Martin, at DTC, discovered this from necessity because his task was to further develop a way of pricing diamonds using modelling – an area of work that he knew nothing about. His boss was clear that he wanted Ian to take on the challenge because he knew a huge amount about the diamond world and pricing in the traditional sense, plus his network of contacts was amazing. So, Ian set out to find the best people and let them know that they would have to teach him where necessary.

Charlotte Butterfield would agree that he was right to go ahead: 'I used to think that I needed to be an expert, but now I manage in accounts and secretarial where I have no experience. You just have to be big enough to ask for advice and keep questioning/looking at the wider picture, asking "What if you do this?", "Have you thought about . . . ?" '

“ You just have to be big enough to ask for advice. ”

Every manager I met talked about getting in people who are either gifted in an area of work or had real talent for the future. It relates back to the issue of focus. Managers who have a balance of self- and other-focus are able to see that:

- ▶ the work and business will benefit from bringing in the very best people
- ▶ it is a real chance to build talent for the organisation and putting them in a fabulous team means that they are more likely to stay
- ▶ such a strong team will deliver terrific results, which will do the manager no end of good, so it is not all altruistic!

So look around the business for the very best people or go outside to the marketplace, just never settle for second best. If you worry that they will show you up or steal your limelight, get some help from an external coach or an internal mentor before it trips you up. Most importantly, remember that *your* job is to manage your people while *they* complete the task – together you will be far more successful than you could ever be on your own.

Action

- ▶ Identify what you see as the risk of employing high performers and consider what you need to do to overcome that.
- ▶ List your own attributes and consider how they will help you to lead the team well.
- ▶ Begin the day by orientating yourself to being a team member who adds a particular piece to the overall outcome.

Managing a difficult team

If you develop a disastrous team, it is likely to have happened in one of three ways:

- you have been asked to take on a team that isn't working, because you are seen as the person who can sort it out
- you take on a team that looks good to begin with. As you get in deeper, the cracks begin to show and you have a problem on your hands
- you have been running a team for a long time and it is OK, but now you want to make it a better place to work.

If you are part of an established team, it can be particularly hard to see the wood for the trees, so don't be afraid to ask for help. I worked with Ian Martin, from DTC, helping him to identify what sort of manager he wanted to be. Exploring old cultural expectations and future business demands enabled him to clarify how to help the team become more innovative and dynamic. When you have a tough job on your hands, for whatever reason, a coach, mentor or colleague with similar experience can be a godsend. So, as soon as you realise what you are facing, find support and use it regularly as you move forward.

When you are clear how you want to move forward, set the new tone for the team:

- Talk them through your plan for the future and invite them to come on board. Be energetic and inviting, painting a picture they can't resist. Above all, make it clear that keeping things the same isn't an option. If you know you are part of the problem, describe what you are doing to change your behaviour, thereby providing a role model for the way forward.
- Meet each person in the team to talk through their options. Prepare for each meeting and get the help you need from your HR department. If you have tough feedback to give, make sure that you have evidence of the issue, be open and honest about the problem and outline what you expect in future.
- Set up regular meetings to check on progress – weekly if necessary. You must indicate that change is essential and give them as much encouragement as you can. Keep notes about progress – this will provide evidence for either celebration or tough action.
- If nothing works, then take action. Don't prevaricate – act as ▶

soon as you possibly can. Any negative energy will pollute the positive work going on in the team.

This isn't an easy job, so keep talking to people who understand. Problems always seem more manageable when shared, so be open and take help wherever you can find it.

Can a manager be friends with direct reports?

This is a thorny one and people have different views. There are two issues to consider:

- Is it right to be friends with the people who report to you?
- How do you manage people who were once your colleagues and friends?

Della Garmory, at Nationwide, feels strongly that you must know your team well and you should get them to know you. She sees the role of manager as one that allows for sharing of personal information when the need arises and she makes sure relationships in the team are open and above board. Because many of her team were colleagues when she was a personnel consultant, she continued with these relationships once she became a manager. However, clear boundaries were set. She is definitely a friend of sorts, but not on a deeply personal level. She keeps that for friends outside work.

❝ Make sure relationships in the team are open and above board. ❞

Oliver Hickson, at COI, had experience of managing his friends. In his first job as a manager he made friends with a couple of colleagues and they supported each other very well. Then Oliver was made head of department, which meant that his two friends had to report to him. They had real difficulty adjusting to him being the boss and he struggled to strike the right note with them. It was a tough time for everyone.

As a result, he learned:

- To set clearly defined roles and responsibilities – this made it easier when he overtly stepped into the manager role and stopped them expecting him to be their 'friend'

▶ To master the art of maintaining an appropriate distance – allowing him to have fun, go to weddings and out for drinks when he wants to. In fact, his team describe him as the 'ringleader' when it comes to fun!

▶ To be a friend at work, but only to the extent that he can have the difficult conversations and be very firm when needed.

So, be friendly and set clear boundaries, but find your own style of doing it. Nic, at Data Connection, aims to build up trust within his team at a professional rather than a personal level. This is because the nature of the work is highly technical and 'fun' for this team lies in the handling of stressful, complex and challenging problems. They all know each other really well in a work setting and do have an occasional drink after work, but mixing work with socialising just isn't a big driver for them.

Action

▶ Think about the relationships you presently have with your team and look for the one that would suit you best.

▶ Set boundaries – be clear when you can be friendly and when you need to be the manager. For example, go to the pub, buy everyone a drink and have a good laugh, but don't get drunk and certainly never speak inappropriately about anyone in the team or the organisation. The word will always get back and you will lose credibility and trust.

▶ Make sure that you can give tough feedback when necessary. If ever you feel worried that someone won't like you, you have crossed the boundary and need to pull back for a while until you re-establish yourself as the *manager*.

Is open plan or a separate office best?

This is a very emotive decision and one that has a major impact on the workplace. There are pros and cons and, depending on what suits your business and culture, different ways to go about it. The options are:

▶ Small groups or individuals sitting in offices. This allows specific groups to bond, but can divide the organisation. This is common in long-established cultures and works fine when silos are an advantage.

▶ The bulk of people are open-plan with the senior managers being allocated personal offices around the edge of the room. They often have glass walls that give an impression of openness but the privacy to do their work. This option is more inclusive, yet also establishes the hierarchy.

▶ Everyone is open-plan including the senior managers. This increases contact across the organisation and reduces the emphasis on hierarchy. Leaders and managers are included in general banter and others get to know something of their work. Offices are available for meetings and quiet time when concentration is needed.

Never mind open plan, Helena Moore, at Bromford Housing Group, feels so strongly about getting in among it with her people that she hot-desks anywhere and everywhere. She even encourages her team to do the same, including Di Beardsmore, the ex-PA to the CEO, who recently joined the team from her safe and consistent office. It was a real change of style and one that she approached with trepidation. However, her trust in Helena was high so she gave it a go and now she really enjoys the variety and chance to meet other people.

Allison Nicoll, at Freedom Finance, is equally determined about sitting with her people because it means that she knows what is going on, can coach them in difficult situations and is on the spot when someone's head goes down. It also means that she can inject some fun when the pressure of endless phone calls gets on top of them.

On the other hand, Tesh Kataria, Oliver Hickson and Andrew Rothesay all sit in offices. They recognise the need to have a space from which to make difficult calls, have conversations that will eventually go back to the team, but not yet, and into which people can come and speak to them privately. They balance the potential for isolation by wandering round on a regular basis. Oliver makes a point of hanging his coat on the hat stand furthest from his office so that he can chat to everyone at the beginning of the day.

So, it is all a matter of taste. Whichever option you choose, make sure that you are easily accessible, which is as much about your facial expression and body language as it is about location. However, if someone has to go out of their way to reach you, that can make it easier to avoid visiting in the tough times, so ensure you and your desk are as easy as possible to approach!

66 Make sure that you are easily accessible. 99

Action
- ▶ Think about how approachable you are. Unless your people can reach you easily and, more importantly, feel able to speak to you when they get there, you are not behaving like an inspirational manager.
- ▶ If you have the option to take down the walls, talk to your people first and make sure that they are all on board. You will probably get some resistance, so listen well to what is said. If you are keen to give open-plan a try, find a way to experiment by sharing rooms or moving into a joint space for a short time.
- ▶ If you are open plan already, include this in your discussions about the team charter and make sure that everyone feels they are being respected. Leave a space in team meetings to find out how people are doing in the physical workspace. This will make it OK for people to have a moan if they need to.

Is my place inside or outside of the team?

Inspirational managers always see themselves as part of the team. They have a senior role in terms of being the manager, but that is merely their job – there are no airs and graces or superiority. They realise that the team can't do its work without the manager, but also that they can't achieve the desired outcomes without the team. So, give some thought to how you see yourself in relation to your people.

Action
- ▶ Make a list of pros and cons. Why should you be part of or not part of the team? Consider the benefits of both in relation to your area of work.
- ▶ Talk with other managers and find out what they think. In particular, look at the managers you admire and see how they work.

➤

119

> ▶ Talk with your own manager and share thoughts about what will best serve the team.

> ▶ For one week, try on for size being an equal person who just has different responsibilities and see how it feels. Get some feedback from your team and use this to identify the right distance for you all.

Managing yourself

As a manager, you will support those who have problems, but at times you will also have to manage your own problems. This happened to Della Garmory when, due to a personal crisis, she had to 'pull in her horns' to manage all the demands on her time. As a result, one person started sinking and Della failed to notice. 'She'd been through a terrible period and I wasn't there – I felt awful.'

Della learned two things from the experience.

▶ 'I shouldn't be that important in the team.' The episode pointed out how dependent people in the team were on her specifically. This created a bottleneck and reduced the degree to which the team members supported each other.

▶ 'I should have realised she was a priority, then I could have left others alone more.' It's a good point – we prioritise work, why not people? Had Della noticed the problem, she would have left those who were doing well and paid more attention where it would make the difference.

When it happens again, she has decided that she will work out who is most needy and buddy them up with someone for the duration. It doesn't need to be her, but there does need to be someone paying attention to them.

Della's team members are also spread to the four winds, so it is not surprising that people tend to rely on her specifically. However your team works – remotely or in the same building – it is worth considering what you will do when a difficult time lands in your lap. How well would others in the team step up to support their colleagues? It is worth talking to your team and putting contingency plans in place – not least because it shows that you are just another member of the team who will also need support from time to time.

Summary

▶ Teams are like family and it is up to you to decide what sort of family you go for.

▶ Once you have gathered the team members, develop a clear charter together and set the tone for the future.

▶ Great teams have strong relationships, so use every opportunity to help people get to know each other better.

▶ If your team members don't work well together, you have to address that. If it means moving people out, it is your job to sort it. To hang back will cost you in terms of the team's performance.

▶ There are many ways to manage a team:

- you don't have to know it all, you can have people who are better than you in the team

- you can be friends, within reason – as long as you can still give the tough messages when the need arises

- office or open-plan arrangements, it is up to you – wherever you are, just make sure that you are really approachable

- better too much communication than not enough, so make sure that you are really easy to access and talk to and that you know what is going on.

Action plan

Problem teams

Today

▶ Write down your concerns about the team and book a discussion with your manager and HR.

Next week

▶ Talk to the team members about the new style and direction for the team.

▶ Arrange one-to-one meetings and begin to gather feedback on individuals.

▶ Hold the meetings as soon as possible.

Next month

▶ Maintain regular one-to-ones to track progress.

121

- Keep making it clear that the status quo isn't an option.
- Make sure you are keeping up the necessary paperwork so you can move people out if you need to.

By the end of three months

- Have moved out the dissenters and have a positive team in place.

Functioning teams

Today

- Mark out time in your diary to think about the sort of team you want.
- Have lunch with anyone in the team who is available and find out how they are doing.

Next week

- Hold a team meeting and create a team charter.
- Be as specific as you can so that everyone understands fully 'how we do things round here'.

Next month

- Set a time to explore the team vision together and agree the next steps.
- Arrange one fun event, having checked out what people would most enjoy.
- Go out for lunch or coffee with one person each week, just for a chat.

CHAPTER

8

The performance management process

'Pick the battles you want to win and those you are prepared to lose.'

Allison Nicoll, Freedom Finance

'Ben always told me when I did things right, but also when I did them wrong. I really appreciate being told, it helps me open my eyes. Over time he's taken me out of my pigeonhole and comfort zone. I have a lot of faith in him now.' So says Andy Summerscales, at Mace, about his one-to-ones with his manager, Ben Wood.

Performance management reminds me of buying clothes. The person who honestly says that I look terrible in an outfit and helps me find the one that works wins my trust. In just the same way, the manager who is totally honest speaks out when things are not going well and then provides support to get it right gains huge credibility. The truth is, people generally know when they are failing, but carry on doing their best in the hope that they will improve before anyone notices. In fact, it is just like wearing the wrong outfit – everyone else can see what is happening – so the sooner problems are dealt with, the better everyone will feel.

Inspirational managers place great store on providing their people with effective performance management. They want their people to know when they are getting it right so that they can enjoy the kudos that brings, but also to support them when the going gets tough so they can use the experience to improve and develop their expertise and strengths. This is the ideal scenario for employees – to know exactly where they stand and how they can be successful.

❝Inspirational managers ... want their people ... to know when they are getting it right ... but also support them when the going gets tough. ❞

125

Performance management feels very demanding

Managing another person is a very demanding task. Returning to the analogy of parenting children, it is the same kind of fun and excitement, but also the same worry and sleepless nights. The big difference is that parents don't have a senior manager checking up on what they are doing, although grandparents may well have an opinion! No wonder, then, that some managers pretend they are actively managing their people while actually keeping their heads down and doing most of the work themselves. There are always plenty of reasons for appraisals and one-to-one meetings not to take place:

- ▶ 'I had this major deadline to meet or I would have had my boss on my back'
- ▶ 'Appraisal time coincides with year-end – HR just don't understand the pressure we are under'
- ▶ 'I filled in the form and sent it back to HR – I think I copied in my direct report'
- ▶ 'I had it in the diary and was all ready for it, then my boss called me for a meeting – you can't expect me to say "No" to her'
- ▶ 'I was sick that day and couldn't do it – the diary's just been too full since then'
- ▶ 'I *will* do it, I just keep forgetting'
- ▶ 'It's HR's job, not mine'
- ▶ 'There was nothing to say really, the work has gone OK'

Even when they do happen, it is not always the best of experiences. Like the person who was in and out in five minutes, having been told 'everything is fine', the manager who spent an hour talking about herself and the business without mentioning her direct report, or the manager who carried on checking his e-mails throughout the meeting. All totally true. No wonder people seek out inspirational managers!

The fact is you can probably get away with it, until there is a real problem. It generally begins with a long-term underperformer who has everyone else picking up after them. Eventually, someone loses their rag and action must be taken.

The obvious first step is to look for evidence of non-delivery in past appraisals, but they show up really well – 'amber/green', 'effective' or 'satisfied all'! It is then exceptionally difficult to act because the underperformer has been led to believe that all was well and their work was good enough or even great. They are totally within their rights to be amazed at poor feedback and the whole process of building up evidence has to begin from scratch.

If you recognise yourself in those examples, don't beat yourself up – just think of all the advantages you can gain by being an inspirational manager and start now to work in that way. Not only will you gain credibility and respect from your people, you will take a real strain off your own back. It is hard to tell the truth and manage talent, but not nearly as tough as worrying that you'll be found out!

Valuing performance management

Effective performance management can make a huge difference to the present and future success of an organisation, yet it is not always highly valued. Even though it is the means by which managers nurture talent, deliver high levels of performance and deal with problems, many businesses place greater emphasis on numbers, targets and outputs. I'm not saying that these are unimportant, just that as one delivers the other, both need quality attention.

The problem is that it can soon become a vicious cycle – that is, if the work of people management is undervalued, managers will concentrate their energies where they get the recognition, which is on the business's outputs. This stops them from allocating time to developing their people, so they have to do more themselves. Which means that they have less time for people management, so they have to downgrade its value in order to validate the choices they are making. The end result is overloaded managers, underdeveloped employees and high-quality 'leavers'.

Appraisal can be an inspirational tool

Charlotte Butterfield, at Badenoch & Clark, is sometimes accused of 'being anal' because she is so keen on detail, but it is part of what enables her to deliver such great results through her team. True, she has the most thorough management process I have heard of and you may feel daunted as you read about it, but just notice how she makes the link between her people and a successful business. Imagine how you would feel if your manager gave this much time to your development, then consider what the achievable equivalent would be with your own people.

All my team have an appraisal each month for a couple of hours and they set the agenda. We talk about their development, their profit and loss, areas of influence, competencies, people development, self-awareness and ways in which they are striving to make a difference – depending on their need at the time. When there are problems to talk through, they know that I expect them to come up with suggestions for what to do. Then we talk about where the problem originated, what they think happened, what they have done to improve this situation and where they need to go from here. If they don't already have an answer, we'll brainstorm together to come up with a good idea. It's really important that they feel properly developed – you don't do anyone any good otherwise.

Everyone also has a six-monthly review to take a more detailed look at their work. This is my special time with them, so we meet at my house for the day. I provide a nice meal and drinks and we talk in depth about work – how they think they are doing, what their ambitions are and what they want to achieve next. It's an exciting time for us both. By the time they leave, I want them feeling energised about the next six months, with a clear idea of what their goals are. It's really important that people feel they have opportunities, their work is looked over and analysed properly and that they have specific goals/aims for the next six months. Getting those outcomes is a really good use of my time.

I always ask how they are as a person. Not many managers do that, but we expect a lot from people and it is important that they feel valued and rewarded. That doesn't just mean financial reward, it also means saying 'thank you'. It's all too easy to finish and just go on to the next thing – I know, I do it myself sometimes. I think about how I'd feel if it was the best month I'd ever had, but no one took much notice. I'd like to tell you I do it all the time but I don't, even though I know how important it is.

The essence of inspirational performance management

The outcome you are looking for is that each of your direct reports is able to do their best work every day of the week. This requires them to understand fully:

- ▶ what their job is – their exact roles, responsibilities and their interdependencies with others
- ▶ how their work contributes to the overall team's outputs
- ▶ the specific outputs that they need to deliver and by when, with significant delivery points or daily targets as appropriate
- ▶ where they have been working really well, with specific examples of their achievements
- ▶ the areas where they need to raise their game and develop
- ▶ how they are doing within the team and as a team member.

When reading this list, you would be forgiven for thinking it could all be put in writing, but that would just be disseminating information – *true* performance management is something quite different. It does include giving information, but it also demonstrates care, challenges thinking and supports change. It is all about a positive and rigorous relationship in which everything can be discussed openly for the good of the employee.

Of course, it is possible to achieve adequate results by telling skilled people what to do and getting out of their way. However, if we are to move into the realms of outstanding performance and exceptional business results, then there is a great deal more to it. This is where inspirational managers come into their own, because they see the job as so much more important than just giving information.

Performance management as a relationship

If you really want the best out of your people, then you have to put that list of information into the context of a relationship. This is what Charlotte is doing when she holds her day-long meetings – making it clear to her people that they are in this together. This works on a number of levels:

- it gives Charlotte an understanding of each person in her team, so she knows what drives and inhibits them
- it ensures that her direct reports get to know her and understand what drives her, which increases the chances of them speaking out when they have a problem
- it provides an environment in which difficult conversations can take place with some degree of comfort and safety
- trust builds over time, bringing with it a desire to please the other, on both sides
- this trust and desire to please extends into team behaviour, including others in the team or work area.

In essence, it is the relationship that makes for exceptional outputs. Once this is in place, a person moves from just earning a crust to wanting to deliver great results, show what they can do and improve the outputs of the team. It brings passion and enthusiasm to the process because, as Della Garmory says, 'relationships are the door to everything'.

Relationships are the door to everything.

Setting up inspirational performance management

So, the inspirational extra in performance management is to build a strong and caring relationship that brings delight, challenge and excitement into the daily workload (Figure 8.1). Everything else is the same, but it is this context that provides the extra zing.

Clear job description,
defined objectives,
timelines   =
+
Relationship

Inspirational
performance
management

Figure 8.1   The formula for inspirational performance management

Building relationships in virtual teams

Building and maintaining good relationships is always easier face-to-face, so leading virtual teams brings an added layer of complexity. However difficult it is, I would really encourage you to meet up at the beginning to establish the relationship, even if it means making a special journey to another venue.

Andrew Rothesay, at Boehringer Ingelheim, manages John McIntosh, who is based in Scotland, so they agree a programme of one-to-one meetings at the beginning of the year and alternate who does the travelling. This is something John really appreciates and it shows how important Andrew thinks he is. Making the effort at the beginning to create a good connection makes it much easier to use the telephone and e-mail when necessary for some communications.

Examples of inspirational performance management

Inspirational managers see performance management as an extremely important part of their job, so put time and energy into making it a positive experience for their direct reports. However, they also all have their own ways of doing it. Let us look at some examples.

Data Connection

At Data Connection, a series of performance management meetings are held.

▶ Each person has a status meeting once a week. This is about tracking designated tasks and ensuring that the work is going to plan.

▶ There is also a lot of spot communication – this is really important for keeping the project on the rails. It is much better to speak straight away rather than wait until the end of the week to find that the project has slipped by two weeks.

▶ There is a nine-month performance management cycle, where the appraisal meeting focuses on personal performance over the past nine months, longer-term capability and areas for development. The latter is built into an individual development plan that focuses on people skills and results in a detailed document written by the manager which includes the salary review. This has a number of stages to it:

1 meeting between the manager and direct report to discuss past performance and future aspirations

2 the manager then writes a report and talks it through with their own manager and senior managers, who add in their feedback

3 the direct report and manager read through and discuss the report to clarify questions or concerns

4 the direct report then has a three-way conversation with their own manager and the manager's manager

5 they then meet with senior leaders to discuss their progress and aspirations.

▶ There is also a more fast-moving document called an individual development plan, or IDP, that is the little brother of the overall review document. It sets out goals for the next three months, for specific actions that are there to drive forward the overall vision that is defined in the review document.

The CEO sees all the review documents, which demonstrates just how important he believes this process to be. Data Connection is a relatively small company, but that doesn't mean that senior-level commitment isn't possible in large organisations – it just means involving the leader one or two levels above the line manager.

Freedom Finance

Charlotte Jennings, Allison Nicoll's manager at Freedom Finance, holds monthly one-to-ones with all her reports. She is very clear that this is their time 'You run it, decide what we need to discuss and we will talk about you and how your work is going.'

As a starting framework, she wants to hear about:

▶ three successes

▶ three 'do differently's'

▶ a look at strengths plus development areas.

This provides a clear starting point and enables a robust discussion about the work. If there are issues that she wants to discuss, she will bring them to the table, but only if the person she is meeting with doesn't do so.

Boehringer Ingelheim (BI)

When people choose their individual contribution towards the overall department or company goals, they will have a lot more buy-in. This is why BI's people set their own objectives and bring them to their managers for discussion. Between them they:

▶ clarify that the objectives and goals are aligned to the company's balanced scorecard

▶ make sure that they are not being overly ambitious

▶ talk through the result they expect to achieve

▶ consider the factors that will help them do it

▶ review the limitations that sit in their way.

Once this has been thrashed out, then the objectives are agreed and documented.

In regular meetings during the year, managers and their direct reports track progress, and if the standards have in fact been set too high, then there is the option to make adjustments as required. However, everyone is given the chance to achieve their chosen goals.

An important part of BI's process is that the company separates development discussions from salary reviews. They have a clear programme for the year, which includes the following.

1 Main performance discussion, which takes place in December/January. The output of this discussion is a clear, forward-looking annual plan of individual objectives linked to the scorecard, projected learning needs/objectives and performance review measures.

2 Bonus is paid in March, based on performance achievements for the previous performance cycle.

3 The annual salary review for all employees takes place in April.

4 In July and August, there is a review of progress against individual objectives/development goals.

5 There is another salary review in October for those employees who have progressed significantly within their role.

Clearly, everyone knows that their performance will determine their bonus and pay award, but splitting the timing takes away that direct connection. There is nothing worse than trying to talk about a problem, knowing that your manager is about to decide on your bonus! Of course it is impossible to ensure that managers aren't influenced by recent happenings, but formally separating the two elements helps to take some of the strain out of it and encourages people to speak their mind when they need to.

The inspirational performance management process

There are three elements to the performance management process:

▶ annual appraisal meeting

▶ monthly one-to-one meetings

▶ ad hoc meetings, as required by a manager or direct reports.

Inspirational managers are not only committed to making these meetings happen, but see them as a major contribution to the success of the team, so they set out to make them a positive experience for their direct reports.

Every element is important because it impacts on whether people see themselves as successful or not. Some people love these meetings, others hate them, but your approach can determine which it is.

The first factor is to make each meeting a priority, only cancelling your appointment in true extremis and always making the new time high priority. I know these different meetings will make a big dent in your diary and you will feel very tempted to look for ways out, but do stick with it. It is a real statement of respect for your team and you may even find that you get to enjoy it, like Charlotte and her day with each team member.

How you manage the discussions will not only impact on the success of the meetings but also your ongoing relationships. If work is going well, then the conversations will be relatively easy, but if there are problems, you need a healthy dose of trust to get a good outcome. This will be built up over time, as you show your commitment to their success and are prepared to do what it takes to help them do their best work.

In each meeting you need to pay attention to two things:

▶ *the content* to ensure that the right data is covered and you both have a chance to put your points of view

▶ *the style* to make this a positive meeting that direct reports look forward to and have faith in.

Annual appraisal meeting

This is a really big deal for a lot of people – particularly those who take their work seriously and even more so when money is tied into it. This is a time to review the year, consider how you worked together and how the relationship needs to move forward in order to achieve the best results. This can only be done in an atmosphere of trust and commitment, so pay attention to the following elements:

Content of the appraisal meeting

Always go into the meeting with a clear plan, having thought through how you want to use the time and the outputs you are looking for. When preparing, remember that there will be two perceptions of the past year – yours and those of your direct reports. The more effective you have been in your performance management over the year, the closer these two perceptions will be and there should be no surprises. However, it is possible that there will be differences, so you need to consider these two viewpoints.

Your direct reports' perceptions of the year

To help with preparation, you might like to give them some 'starter' questions to focus their thinking.

- ▶ How do you feel about work at present – what are you enjoying and what causes you angst?
- ▶ Are there any particular pressures it would help me to know about – are you are having a tough time with children, parents, health? (You can then look for ways to support them to continue to work well. Parents have often told me that having an understanding manager when the kids were sick has really improved their commitment. If they don't want to tell you, accept it, but at least they know you care and they may decide to talk with you in future.)
- ▶ What do you think is going really well with your work and why? How have you delivered on your set objectives?
- ▶ Are there areas where you feel that you need to develop your skills and abilities further?
- ▶ Are there any problems you are facing? What is causing them? What needs to happen in order to move forward?

Your own perceptions of the year

Gather data about your team members' performance prior to the meeting and think through the feedback you want to give them. Begin by talking to colleagues they have worked with over the year to gather their thoughts on effectiveness, successes and problems, paying particular attention to any dotted line reporting relationships.

Then think about your own experience of working with them – both in terms of deliverables and relationships. Let's be clear, this is definitely *not* the moment to speak about how they let you down in a meeting six months ago. It is a very poor manager who saves feedback for an appraisal meeting. In fact, if you are doing your job well, there will be no surprises.

Summarise your feedback under the following headings:

▶ successes over the year – what they achieved and the impact this had

▶ feedback you want to give about their personal attitude and approach

▶ any problems and how well you worked together to sort them out, with ideas for how you might improve this further

▶ define what you see as their main talents and how you think they can build on this further – put your talent scout hat on and think about it in terms of future opportunities in the business

▶ any steps you think need to be put in place for ongoing development.

Style of the appraisal meeting

Find a comfortable and pleasant environment for the meeting if you can, but at least make sure that it is away from the general hum of the office and make it clear to everyone else that this is special time that can only be interrupted in a real emergency. It is likely that the other members of the team will respect this as they will want their own time in the future.

Encourage your direct reports to talk about their experiences and concerns and go into full listening mode, asking questions to clarify your understanding when necessary. Keep your thoughts to yourself until you have heard what they have to say and resist being defensive. Remember, this is *their* perception of the year, so it is totally true for them, even if it doesn't fit with your own. Reflect back what you have heard them say so that they can correct you if you have misunderstood. Once you are totally clear, talk them through the year from your perspective and have a discussion about any differences. Hopefully the perceptions are pretty much in line with each other, but if you do discover major variation, then you clearly need more robust one-to-one meetings in the forthcoming year. When performance management is going well, there should be no surprises at appraisal.

Keep notes as you go along, including any agreements made or else invite your direct report to write them, so that they understand they have an active part to play in the process. You can then use these notes as the basis for a written summary, but make sure you send nothing through to your boss/HR until your direct report has seen it first and agreed with what you have said. You can have the best conversations in the world, but if you follow them with 'secret' statements, you risk creating suspicion and losing trust.

Monthly one-to-one meetings

These are where the feeling of overload is likely to raise its head. Most managers are prepared for the idea of appraisal and, even if they don't get around to it, at least they know it is expected. The frequency of one-to-one meetings is often left to the discretion of managers, but it is this that will make the difference between OK and inspirational managers. If there is one thing I've learned in my time coaching managers/leaders and working with those who have high potential, it is that even the most compelling message gets lost in the mass of daily demands. However brilliant your appraisal meeting and however keen people are to deliver on their objectives, when they get back to their desks and a load of e-mails, their enthusiasm will be dented. The one-to-ones help them stay on track because they know that they will have to update you on progress.

❝ Even the most compelling message gets lost in ... daily demands. ❞

Content of one-to-one meetings

The purpose of this meeting is to keep track of the day-to-day work and ensure that it is in line with the annual objectives, as well as keeping up to date with personal development and any problems as they arise. To achieve this, include the following areas in your discussion.

▶ Check generally how work is going. If you know that things are happening at home, show some interest. Asking how the school play went or if the new car's as racy as hoped shows you care, so don't skimp on this one.

▶ Revisit the business objectives set in the appraisal meeting, be specific and talk through each area. Congratulate them on their achievements and talk through any difficulties, finding out how you can help. Decide on some actions together and make sure that you can deliver on any promises made.

▶ Look back at the development plan you agreed at appraisal time and talk through how it is going. If training was planned, make sure that it is on track and give any help needed to make it happen. Add in new ideas or opportunities you have spotted and give feedback on changes you have observed.

▶ Talk about your relationship and find out if you are giving them the support they need. Find out how else you may be able to help them and be ready to listen, even if the feedback is hard. You expect them to take the tough message, so make sure you model that yourself.

Style of one-to-one meetings

The style of this meeting is as important as for the appraisal, although there is the option to be a bit more informal in one-to-ones. Paul Dunmore, at Thomson Directories, sometimes has this conversation in the car going to a meeting or over a cup of coffee. If you work remotely from your people, then this may be one you can do over the phone, although I would encourage you to meet face to face whenever you can. The important thing is to treat this as valuable time together and not allow it to be interrupted unless absolutely necessary. Then, they will look forward to these meetings, not dread them!

Ad hoc meetings

This is about being available when someone needs you. If you expect people to wait for formal meetings to discuss issues, then you are asking for trouble. It would be fine if you could control the customers, market and suppliers or persuade them only to make a fuss when you are due to meet, but I don't fancy your chances. In which case, you need to be available when the need arises.

❝You need to be available when the need arises.❞

Content of ad hoc meetings

Your reports need to know that they can speak to you at any point if they really need to. There may be a problem with a customer that needs immediate attention if you are not to damage this all-important relationship or it may be that they have a great idea for how to improve the work process that will save much-needed time. Either way, making them wait will be a loss to the organisation. Equally, you may need to update them on some information from your own boss or give them important feedback about their effectiveness and impact. Again, it would be a great mistake to delay having these conversations.

Style of ad hoc meetings

By their nature, these meetings can't be planned. You may only have five minutes to spare or your direct report may be on such a tight deadline that they need a quick answer and go.

The main feature of style here is that you need to give all your attention, even when you feel rushed, under pressure or just a bit low. Make it clear how much time you have and on hearing the issue, make a judgement call about the relative importance of this against your own workload.

If you really believe that you don't have time for ad hoc discussions, think about Fran Rodgers and her team at Northampton Borough Council who have the unenviable task of turning around an ailing council. As Fran says, 'When you are eating the elephant, everyone needs support.' She has moved her desk to be nearer to two of her direct reports just so she can pick up more and throw in a word of encouragement when needed. In truth, every day is busy in the extreme, but she makes clear to her people that she will always find five minutes if they really need her. However, she also makes a point of saying if she thinks that they could have handled it themselves – not as a criticism, but as a way of encouraging them to take on responsibility.

Open door – true or false?

'No problem there – I already have an open door policy, so I'm always available.'

Most managers certainly *aim* to have a *real* open door. It is a great idea and, when it works well, is fantastic for your team, although pretty demanding for you. However, I would encourage you to have a think about the overall message you give from your desk. I have seen managers sitting inside their offices with their 'open doors', head down with just a frowning brow on view and a huge pile of papers surrounding them. Who on earth would walk in there?

Of course, we all have tough days when we are truly under the cosh and it is very hard to be interrupted. The trick is to handle your own work and still be available when people have problems. The last thing you want as a manager is for people to struggle on alone when a bit of help would either avert the problem or reduce the time it steals.

Different managers have all sorts of agreements with their people:

▶ an open door says 'feel free to come in', but a closed door says 'I don't want to be interrupted unless there is an emergency'

▶ some people have an object that sits on the top of their computer when they are concentrating and do not want to be interrupted.

▶ one person I met wears a baseball cap when too busy to speak.

Talk with your team members and find a way to define when you are available and where the boundaries of their responsibilities lie, so they know when to speak and when to make their own decisions. Agree a method and try it out over a couple of weeks. You can then find out how it has worked in a team meeting and see if you need to adjust the process.

This may sound a bit laborious, but it will pay off. Not everyone finds it easy to walk in on the boss and ask for help – it can be a bit like going to the headteacher's office. If you speak about it openly, making it clear that you really are available and what you will say if you're not, then it will be much easier for everyone to approach you when necessary.

141

Limit the number of direct reports

By now it will be very clear that inspirational performance management is an intensive process and you will only be truly successful if you have time to give to your people. This means limiting the number of people you are responsible for. The suggested number varies according to the organisation, but everyone I met considered nine to be over the top.

So, if you feel that you are fighting a losing battle with a team of 15 or more, see what you can do to reduce your load. Show your manager this chapter and talk through the options: you can do a mediocre job with too many people or reduce the load and do an inspirational job for some. Look for creative ways to manage this and keep in mind personal development for the team as you discuss it. I realise this won't be easy, especially in organisations that have a flat structure, but it is worth the effort – it will make a big difference to the quality of your performance management.

❝ Reduce the load and do an inspirational job. ❞

At Data Connection, they set a limit at one direct report for each finger on your hand. Nic divides his time roughly into three days per week with his team and two days a week on his own work. Because the work is so highly skilled, it is considered really important that managers can do everything the team does because this is what will gain the respect of such bright, techie people. It is also clear that these people require a lot of time and plenty of opportunity to talk about the work at hand and how they are doing, hence their phrase, 'high-tech, high touch'.

I realise that this will sound totally unrealistic to many readers, so I asked Helena Moore, at Bromford Housing Group, about her time allocation with regard to management and this was her answer:

> I went to a presentation by BMW and I know the ratios they gave it were that 90 per cent of time should be on leadership and management and 10 per cent doing … jealous or what!

I really do think managers have a huge challenge, so my top tips would be these.

▶ Block out planning time in your diary, preferably out of the office, and turn off the mobile! Even with a 'Please, please, please do not disturb me' on the door, people can't resist the 'Can I just ask you this … it's only a quickie.' I know because I do this to my manager!

▶ Seize the moment – if something comes up that would benefit from management action, do it then and there, e.g. the 'thank you' in person, a handwritten card highlighting something great …

▶ Don't think you can't do some of the day job when managing – sitting among the team and getting a first-hand feel for what is going on means you can multitask managing and day-to-day work … even blokes can multitask on this one! (Not very PC I know, but I am the first to admit that I have to drive up the page on a map!)

So, in short, vanish when you need to plan, cash in on the moment and cheat by multitasking it!

Summary

▶ It is tempting to put performance management at the bottom of your 'to do' list. It is a lot of work, but it will pay off in spades if you give it the time it needs.

▶ If you do your appraisals and one-to-one meetings well, people will look forward to them. They are special times in the management relationship. Your people will appreciate the time and attention you show them and it will increase their commitment to doing a good job.

▶ This is about getting clear on responsibilities, contribution, deliverables and learning needs. It is also about building strong relationships.

▶ Great managers hold:

– appraisal meetings every 6 or 12 months

– one-to-one meetings monthly

– ad hoc meetings as necessary.

▶ To provide truly inspirational performance management, you need to have a manageable number of direct reports.

Action plan

Today

▶ Clarify when you have to do the next appraisals and work out a plan of action, including gathering feedback ahead of time from others your reports have worked with. Make sure that you don't leave this to the last minute – give yourself time to do it properly.

Next week

▶ Set time aside in the diary for your one-to-one meetings. Make sure that you will see every team member in the near future.

▶ Hold at least one meeting this week.

Next month

▶ Identify a manager who is really good at holding appraisal and one-to-one meetings. Ask them for some time and find out how they approach it.

▶ Ask your team for feedback on the one-to-one meetings you have held. Talk this through in your own one-to-one meeting with your manager and look for ways to improve.

CHAPTER

9

Making the most of delegation

'Find time for the people stuff *every day*.'

Helena Moore, *Bromford Housing Group*

In the 'management as chore' scenario, delegation is the way to pass on work. The team becomes a dumping ground for boring tasks that don't bring any kudos, and, at worst, they do the work while the manager takes the glory. In the 'noble art' of management, however, delegation is the key to making the best of strengths, talent and enthusiasm. It not only provides people with interesting challenges, but leaves you with time to support them.

Most managers fall somewhere between these two extremes, fluctuating between handing on work effectively and preferring to do it themselves – the 'give it to me syndrome' (normally accompanied by a martyred sigh!). Inspirational managers enjoy delegating well because it gives them time to develop their people, which they love doing, and role models the positive behaviour of honesty, openness and fairness.

What is delegation?

When done properly, delegation is an amazing development tool in its own right. It involves:

▶ choosing pieces of work that will stretch team members and provide them with opportunities to develop strengths to the next stage

▶ handing on work to prepare people for the next steps in their careers

▶ providing interesting challenges for team members who have reached the height of their careers to ensure that work remains interesting.

Approaching delegation in this way explodes the long-held myth that it will free up your time. In fact, it just changes what you do because, as soon as you delegate, you will need time to coach, teach and supervise. We are not talking abdication, we are talking a partnership that delivers strong results *and* builds succession at the same time. A win–win for the organisation, it demonstrates clearly just how important the role of inspirational manager is to the success of a business.

" A partnership that delivers strong results and builds succession. "

Learning the art of management through delegation

At Data Connection they use positive delegation to develop their managers. Anyone who expresses an interest or who is thought to have a talent for management follows a set procedure:

1 The aspiring manager is assigned as a mentor with no direct responsibility for quality of work, team behaviour and so on. They spend time together talking about the mentee's work, sharing ideas and challenging thinking. It gives the mentee access to support from a senior expert and enables the mentor to see if they like working with people. Managers gather feedback on the effectiveness and style of the mentor from the mentee and hold weekly meetings with the mentor to find out how it is going and whether or not they are enjoying the process.

2 If the mentor wants to continue exploring their appetite for management, they prepare by attending a 'New Manager Briefing' run by Ian Ferguson, the chairman, where he takes them through the management ethos of Data Connection. They talk through relevant policies, do role-plays together and go away with a raft of relevant documents to read.

3 The new manager is then allocated one direct report. This management work is directly linked to their Individual Development Plan and includes daily contact with their own manager and regular feedback from their direct report on effectiveness and style. As the new manager becomes more confident and familiar with the demands, they are given more scope and report in less often.

4 When feedback is consistently positive and the new manager is enjoying their work, they will be given more people to manage, up to the agreed level of five – 'one for each finger on your hand'. Even when this level is reached, the manager's own one-to-ones will include time to discuss how their management work is going.

Not only is this a fantastic example of delegation, it is wonderful preparation for management. If only all new managers were looked after so well!

Assess your workload

A first step in delegation is to decide which pieces of work can be passed on to your direct reports. To do this, you need to assess your task list to identify:

▶ what must be done by you

▶ what can be delegated to experts in your team

▶ what can be delegated as a development opportunity.

Workloads vary from one manager to another: some are primarily managing their teams, some have workloads that match those of their direct reports, while others cover a different work area from that of the people in their team.

Whatever the situation, your job as an inspirational manager is to ensure that each person is doing the work that suits their strengths and talents, that the tasks are providing the best development opportunities to the right people and you have enough time in your week to manage these people effectively.

❝ Ensure that each person is doing the work that suits their strengths and talents. ❞

It is really helpful to review your workload periodically to see if you are spending your time in the most productive manner or if there are tasks that can be done better by others.

Action

▶ Map out the responsibilities of the team on a large sheet of paper and show the linkages between each person, plus their strengths and aspirations.

▶ Consider whether the current allocation of work fits people's talents and aspirations and will help them develop their abilities. If you don't know what their aspirations are, plan a meeting to create a development plan with them.

▶ Put your own work on the map, including your strengths and ➤

---

aspirations, then mark those tasks that have to remain your responsibility and the tasks that can be handed on.

▶ Using your judgement and knowledge of your people, identify which pieces of work can be handed over, either as development or because the person is capable of doing them.

▶ Once you have a clear picture of what can be delegated, discuss the workloads of the receivers and see what they can hand on for someone else's development.

▶ Mark time in your diary to manage this process. If you are suggesting that someone in the team hands on work to a junior, decide if you will manage it or whether it is an opportunity for management development for a team member along the lines of the process in place at Data Connection.

▶ Talk your conclusions through with your boss.

Keep in mind that you need to find the right balance for time spent on tasks and time spent on people. For example, Nic Larkin, at Data Connection, has three direct reports and splits the week into three days on management and coaching and two days on task. Unless you allocate specific amounts of time to these things, there is a real risk that people management will be squeezed in where you don't have anything more important to do. That is a short cut to problems!

The process of delegation

Inspirational managers give quality time to delegation and the end result is increased peace of mind. It can feel risky handing on work to people who are not used to doing it, knowing that the results will impact on the team outputs. You are responsible, but you are not doing the work and if it goes wrong, the buck stops with you which can feel a bit like a poisoned chalice. On the upside, it is an exciting adventure in developing talent.

Here are some basic rules that will make sure you see the upside and enjoy the ride.

Make time

Please don't get sucked into the common assumption that you are giving your work away to another person because there is no doubt that delegation takes time. If you understand this, you will make space in your diary for check-in meetings and coaching discussions. If you don't, problems will land on your desk and eat up more time than it would take to do the work yourself, which is why so many managers end up doing just that!

You need to consider delegated work a joint effort, especially in the early days, with you retaining responsibility for the outputs even though you are not doing the bulk of the work. So, asking someone to take on a task and then turning your back is not an option. It is counterproductive and unwise.

" Consider delegated work a joint effort. "

Give clear instructions and guidelines

When delegating a task, give as much information as you can.

▶ Sit down together and discuss the whole task, making sure that the person understands what is expected of them.

▶ Be clear about objectives, expectations, timelines and measurements that relate to the work. There is nothing more disheartening than putting in a lot of work and then finding that your boss didn't want it done that way.

▶ Arrange a meeting after a couple of days when the person has had time to think about the specific piece of work – by then questions will be clearer and more informed.

▶ Talk about the impact on the rest of the person's workload to clarify the demands and expectations that have been placed on them. Find out how you can help them reorganise appropriately.

Arrange follow-up meetings at the outset

You need to meet with the person taking on the delegated task on a regular basis. These discussions have a two-fold purpose.

▶ To challenge thinking, provide support and track progress on the delegated work. This ensures greatest personal development and business output.

▶ To provide you with information about how the work is progressing, the obstacles that are encountered and impact on people in other parts of the business. This takes care of the fact that the work still belongs to you and leaves you able to answer questions whenever they arise.

As the person becomes more proficient in the task, the amount of time it takes will reduce and, if they are very able, it may only need a monthly meeting. Whatever it takes, though, make sure that you have it in your diary as soon as the work is handed on and you will reduce the chances of problems taking you by surprise. You will most certainly still also need to give time on an ad hoc basis, because requirements will change, but at least you will be fully up to date when they do.

Tell the truth

Inspirational managers make a point of telling the truth. They know that there is little value in letting people think that they are doing a good job when, in fact, the outputs are not up to standard. If you leave them to struggle, you make your job even harder because everyone else knows, so you lose credibility and the person is given no chance to improve. So, as soon as you realise that there is a problem, discuss:

▶ what happened to cause the difficulty

▶ identify where the root of the problem lies

▶ look at the options

▶ make a rescue plan together that will bring them and the work back on track.

The same applies when the work is good and you are impressed with their performance. Make a big deal of it in a way that shows them how much you appreciate the efforts that they have made and, if appropriate, tell other people what a good job they have done. Always take into account the personality of the person concerned so that your actions feel positive, not embarrassing. When done well, there is nothing better than a 'thank you' for effort and outputs – it does the world of good.

> ❝ When done well, there is nothing better than a 'thank you' ❞

Learning from your own mistakes

Telling the truth is key to any form of personal development, delegation included, but you need to tell it in a way that enables people to take it in and make the most of the opportunity it presents. As Della Garmory, at Nationwide, says:

> When you make a mistake with an individual, it's hard to go back and put it right. You really have to work at it. If you have misjudged something or someone, causing upset and possibly conflict, it takes a lot to get that trust back again.

> I had a member of staff who joined my high-performing team feeling very confident. However, I realised that the experiences she would be exposed to in this new job would show up a number of gaps.

> I'd got used to managing the team and knew them all very well, so I made the mistake of just launching in. I talked about the development path of the existing team as a way of demonstrating the steep learning curve she was on, but what she heard me say was 'There's a big gap between you and this existing team, so there's a lot for you to do.'

> In fact, it is what I needed to say, but it was too soon, because I didn't have the relationship. She became very defensive and it was a tearful conversation – I felt really bad. I reflected hard that night and spoke to her next day to apologise. I didn't apologise for what I said, but for not considering the timing of this conversation. I also expressed my concern that the conversation could have felt really demotivating for someone joining a new team.

➤

It was really tough to hear what came next. It seems she had never felt so demotivated after leaving a one-to-one with a manager before and had *never* had anybody tell me that, so it was a mutual feeling. She'd felt judged without having been given a chance. She started to recognise that she may not have as much experience, but that's why she was joining the team in the first place. The positive side was that she felt I really did want to help her.

Looking back, it was a combination of things – I had become complacent because the team had been settled for so long. Plus, I was feeling urgent – we had lost some experience in the team, so I really did need the gap filled quickly.

The learning?

▶ If you take a new person into a high-performing team, you have to go right back to the beginning and build up the new team.

▶ Never be complacent and expect them to pick up the team norms.

▶ Better still, use them to identify the gaps, so you can improve the team even further.

Making the best use of mistakes

The manager who uses mistakes well is destined for greatness. Show me a person who doesn't make mistakes and I'll show you someone stuck in a rut and not achieving. Inspirational managers are peoplebuilders and you will never build a strong performer without any mistakes, so don't even expect it. In fact, if you haven't had to deal with any mistakes lately, I would take a good look at how creative and dynamic your team is being. The last thing you want is for problems to be hidden away.

" The manager who uses mistakes well is destined for greatness. "

Mistakes you make

Everyone makes them, so don't beat yourself up the first time you get it wrong as an inspirational manager. If you keep making the *same* mistake, then feel free! Because people are so complex, it is inevitable that the life of a manager will run a bumpy course. As each mistake comes back to bite you, take time to think it through and sort out what you need to do to put it right. As Della Garmory says, you are likely to have lost a bit of trust, so think about how to rebuild it.

Most important of all, feel free to apologise. Paradoxically, it can earn you more credibility than if you had never made the mistake in the first place. I once coached a CEO who made an unfortunate statement in a large group meeting. New to the company, he realised that he had been too abrupt for the prevailing culture and his first instinct was to go straight back and apologise, but he was told 'that's not how we do things round here'. As time went on, he realised that it was still lurking in the shadows and he wasn't building the relationships he needed. After our discussion, he decided to send out an e-mail referring to his gaff and saying how sorry he was to have offended in that way. Contrary to popular opinion, it made a major difference to how people saw him. They were impressed with his courage and sensitivity and it set a new norm in the culture.

❝ Feel free to apologise. ❞

If the mistake is only partly to do with you or if responsibility is cloudy, don't get picky, take it on the chin and lead the way. Set an example, making it clear that it is OK to make mistakes. This will do more to encourage others to speak out than anything else you could say or do.

Making the most of mistakes

According to Oliver Hickson, at COI, it is good to make mistakes, but he is very clear that it is 'really bad to give people a hard time when they do. I mean, admittedly, if they make the same mistake ten times in a row you might get a bit annoyed, but it is good for people to make and learn from mistakes.'

➤

He gave an example of some proofreading that went very wrong. A booklet was being prepared to go out to schools on drug use and the classification section ended up naming everything as Class A. Fortunately it hadn't yet been distributed when the mistake was spotted, but it had to be reprinted, which cost a lot of money.

Richard looked into what had gone wrong and brought it to a team meeting so we could talk through it to identify best practice for the future. In this instance, the client hadn't got us involved enough, and since we were busy and not being paid a great amount, we let it go. In the future, the client needs to decide if they want us involved or not and, if they do, to pay a fair fee so we can afford to give the time it needs. So, yes, it was a mistake, but good learning for us all.

Oliver makes sure that the team members discuss mistakes and the learning they bring – there is no hiding away in a darkened room here! 'We have a really good team dynamic, so people see it in the right light and take learning from it themselves. Anyway, people on the team would have seen the poor guy tearing his hair out, so, actually, they end up empathising.

Mistakes other people make

There are two issues here:

▶ you want your people to speak out as soon as they realise that there has been a mistake

▶ you need them not to make the same mistake again.

Tesh Kataria, at Tower Homes, makes a point of including everyone in learning about mistakes. To his mind, the team always works better together, celebrating successes and dealing with mistakes. However, this is nothing to do with laying blame. To begin with, he meets with the team member concerned to:

▶ talk the situation through to understand what happened

▶ come up with a rescue plan together

▶ review what happened to take the learning for next time

▶ amend team procedures to make sure any new people don't make the same mistake.

The next step is to bring the issue to the team alongside new ideas, congratulations and other learning. He doesn't name the person, but it does bring a clear message that mistakes are not terminal and we all learn a huge amount from them.

Handling a mistake

As soon as a mistake comes to your attention arrange a time to discuss it with the person concerned. Do this as soon as you can – remember, the person may feel anxious about your reaction, in which case they will be distracted and this will affect their other work.

Don't wade straight in with your frustrations and instructions about what they should have done differently. You never know, they might have done really well in a tough situation and ploughing in will just cost you their trust.

Action

▶ Listen carefully to find out exactly what happened. What were the circumstances and who was involved?

▶ Explore whether or not the person had seen it coming and, if so, what they had done to avert it.

▶ Understand all the different factors that were involved, including customers, other teams, managers, suppliers and so on.

▶ Hear where the person thinks they went wrong and the significant contributory factors.

▶ Develop a plan of action that will sort out the problem and find a way to rescue the reputation of the person or the team as appropriate. As a matter of urgency, you have to deal with the business reality.

Once the plan is in place and those actions that can be taken are done spend time with your direct report, looking at the learning. Include your own contribution to the mistake – delegation is a partnership, so you are sure to have played your part, even if it was through absence. Use this as a way of increasing your understanding of what the person might need in the future.

Coach your team member to explore what they could have done differently. Your main task now is to ensure that your direct report learns all he or she can from the experience and understands how to stop it happening again. Also, look for general learning that will help them with their development.

If you can come out of this discussion without having to lay down the law and tell your report what to do, you have done an excellent job!

However, if the same mistakes keep recurring, then you must act.

▶ Once is fine and can be managed.

▶ Twice is cause for concern.

▶ Three times needs very serious thought.

When a problem does keep recurring, you need to consider whether the person has been promoted beyond their capabilities or if this part of the job is just beyond them, while other areas are OK. If the mistakes reinforce other concerns, then you must make the tough decision and decide if they are right for the job.

Summary

▶ Delegation is the ideal way to develop your people, which means that you must use the time it releases to support them.

▶ Delegating is particularly good for growing new managers.

▶ Take time out to assess your workload. Are you doing work that others could do or that would provide a good development opportunity?

▶ There are four rules of positive delegation:

– give time to the process

– give clear instructions and guidelines

– arrange follow-up on meetings at the outset

– tell the truth at all times.

➤

- Mistakes are really valuable and help people learn. Always talk them through to understand what happened and how to do it differently next time.

- Be honest about your own mistakes. You earn trust by telling the truth and set a good role model by talking about what you have learned.

- When others make a mistake, take time as soon as you can to explore the mistake with the person concerned in order to maximise their learning.

- If mistakes keep happening, take action.

Action plan

Today

- Map out your present workload in terms of tasks and people or book out a time within the next two weeks to do this.

- If your diary is so full it looks impossible, identify what you can cancel: your workload has obviously reached crisis point so you need to do this assessment as soon as possible.

Next week

- Allocate times over the next month when you can meet with each team member to produce or review their development plans. This will help you to allocate work more appropriately.

- List the work you have already delegated and review how the tasks are progressing. If you don't know, work out what you need to know and what stage you expect the work to have reached. Write a list of the possible obstacles and difficulties that might be encountered.

- Meet with at least one person who has a delegated task and get up to date with the work. Do this in a coaching style and help them explore the issues that face them. Remember, you are a partner, not just there to instruct.

- Put times in the diary to see the other people as soon as possible.

Next month

- Make sure that you have completed your workload assessment. If you can't see what to hand on, take the map to your own one-to-one with your manager and decide on priorities together.

▶ Work out a plan of action for the handover of work. Set yourself a deadline for handing over the agreed amount of work. If you don't do this, you will end up carrying on as usual.

▶ Pay attention to your own mistakes and those of your team. Find a way to celebrate the learning that comes from them so everyone understands that mistakes are not the end of the world but the sign of a dynamic and creative team.

CHAPTER

10

Managing your talent

'Believe in your people, then they will do things that they haven't done before.'

Helena Moore, Bromford Housing Group

Now we are into the really exciting bit – spotting talent and helping people to grow. Maurice Purslow works for Andrew Rothesay at Boehringer Ingelheim now, but his first contact was as his mentor – in fact, he mentored Andrew into his present role. When Andrew was promoted, Maurice still acted as his mentor alongside becoming his direct report: 'It's wonderful to be managed by him now – he still asks for my opinion and vice versa.'

Not everyone would be OK with such a complex relationship, but if you want to be a great talent manager, accept it as your badge of honour! It is the perfect statement of balanced focus when you are so thrilled to see another advance beyond you. It is an accolade to Maurice that he can do it and equally to Andrew that he has created such a positive relationship as manager: 'We appreciate each other's strengths so we just worked at keeping the same relationship.'

Maurice told me, 'I relish my appraisal time. Andrew knows I put in 120 per cent and makes me feel really valued. We don't just talk about my work, but the company and where it's going. We have a symbiotic relationship really and he involves me in strategic and change work, which keeps me going. He always knows when I'm down – I can be a bit emotional, so give away what I'm feeling. Andrew rings me on a Friday night to talk about the week and say "Well done", which often leads on to a few drinks.'

Stages of talent management

So how do you go about spotting talent? There are several steps you need to follow.

▶ Develop your talent-spotting muscle. Look at each person who works for you or that you are recruiting with the next three jobs in mind.

▶ Know your people's aspirations. Find out what each person in your team aspires to – job progression or otherwise. Unless you understand their ambitions and desires, you won't spot the opportunities as they arise.

▶ Build your manager network. Keep in touch with other managers on a regular basis so you are clear about the possibilities across the business that will help your people.

▶ Expect the best. As soon as you spot talent and know the person is up for it, be prepared to drive, push and cajole. Stretch is never easy, so be ready for hiccups.

▶ Celebrate with them when they achieve and enjoy your success.

“Stretch is never easy, so be ready for hiccups.”

Look for talent everywhere

Terry Woodcock joined Tower Homes in the central admin. office and his first task was to collect and drop off the post. A bright lad, he wasn't satisfied with just doing the job – he always made an effort to talk with people and find out what they were doing. He was full of curiosity – something Tesh spotted early on. When necessary, he would speak on the phone to customers and was really keen to help, so having checked that his hunch about Terry's ambitions was correct, Tesh created a grade three role so that he could do some admin. work.

To help him get to grips with the job:

▶ Tesh sat beside him whenever he could and listened in on the calls he was making. This gave him the opportunity to coach Terry on how to improve and move towards the conclusion he wanted. These times were intense at first and then the gap between got longer. After 12 months, Terry excelled.

▶ Tesh then arranged a two-hour session each day with another member of the team, going through the eight stages of the team process. This took place once he had finished his own work, so gave him a real incentive to finish and get into the learning.

As soon as the next appropriate vacancy came up, Terry applied and got the job. Now he is a star in the team and has been working as a grade five for the past three years. He recently let out 25 apartments to key workers, got a 9 out of 10 rating for his customer service, has been Employee ➤

of the Quarter and got the Outstanding Achievement Award at the London and Quadrant conference. How's that for talent-spotting?

If we look back at the metaphor of family, this is like supporting your children to fulfil their dreams. You are not in competition and you afford them your time and effort because you want to see them succeed. Great managers take a similar approach. And it's not all altruistic. Tesh has taken great delight in Terry's achievement and it has done no end of good for his reputation as a manager. A win–win situation all round.

So, let's look at the steps for spotting talent one at a time.

Develop your talent-spotting muscle

This is about refining your Other-Focus. If you want to get into talent-spotting, start now assuming that nothing is as it seems. Don't be satisfied with the obvious and think twice about what you see or what people tell you. This isn't about doubting in a negative way rather looking for the hidden strengths and career aspirations that people might not think they can tell you or might take for granted themselves.

▶ Pay attention to what people do well and see how you can stretch that ability in them.

▶ Notice the subjects that get people fired up.

▶ If you suspect that someone will be good in a particular role, talk to them about it.

▶ Follow hunches and try out the ones you suspect will be good.

Charlotte Butterfield, at Badenoch & Clark, had a moody girl in her team that her own manager thought she should be moved out. However, Charlotte believed in her and didn't want to give up, so she put time into listening and getting to know her, motivating her until the girl herself believed that she was good enough. She also gave her a very clear structure and goals to work to. It took her a while to raise her game, but she is now a top biller.

Action

▶ Go through the people in your team. Where do you think the talent lies? Have you talked with these people to check what they are looking for careerwise? If not, book some time for a one-to-one with them and find out.

▶ Of those you dismissed in your first thoughts, think about how they are performing. If they are just a bit lacklustre, it may be that they are bored. So focus on their strengths, work out what will inspire them and take appropriate action.

▶ Consider the direction of the organisation, the vision and key strategic needs. What does this mean for your area of the business? What skills and talents will you need over the next couple of years if you are to deliver exceptionally well? This gives you an idea of the talent you need to nurture in the near future. Keep this in mind as you read the next steps.

Know your people's aspirations

This is the balancing plank to your own hunches and observations. Make sure that you have regular conversations with your direct reports about where they want to go in their career.

▶ First you will discover those who are ambitious and want to develop a career path that suits their skills. This means that you can be clear about the possibilities and develop a plan of action.

▶ Second, and less easy is finding the ones who could be more ambitious, but presently hide their light under a bushel.

▶ Third, harder again, you will find the ones whose aspirations run beyond their talent, but at least now you can manage their expectations.

▶ Fourth, you will also identify those who love their work as it is and have no aspirations whatsoever to progress. Again, you need to know about this so that you can keep them motivated and challenged even when they are doing the same job over a long period of time.

Action

Arrange to sit down with each team member for a career discussion. Give warning of the subject matter because some people will be excited and want to prepare, but others will assume that you are going to give them bad news.

▶ Explain that you want to help them develop their talents, whether that means preparing for promotion or finding the best way to do their present job.

▶ Listen carefully to what they are saying. Ask open questions that require more than just 'Yes' or 'No' answers – 'Can you tell me a bit more about that?', 'Can you explain what you mean?' and so on. Make notes to remind you of the details. *See also Chapter 6.*

▶ When you understand fully, tell them your thoughts. Remember, just because you haven't seen a trait yet doesn't mean that it is not there, so, if you are not sure, support them to explore the possibilities.

▶ Work out a plan of action together – strengths and how they can be built on, areas for development and how to address them, plus clearly defined objectives and timelines.

If you are only just getting to grips with your talent-spotting muscle, there are several things that you can do. First of all, take the anxiety out of it by explaining to your people that this is new to you, but no less important for that. Prepare in advance the questions you want to ask, the feedback you want to give about where they are strong and where they need to develop, and your thoughts on their work so far. Finally, as you won't get it right first time, ask for feedback. By doing this, you also set a great example of developing and learning from experience.

Talent management really is part of your job!

Of course, you do have to deliver on targets and your own work is important, but you are also central to the drive for strong succession in the organisation. All too often, succession is seen as being the domain of those in the upper echelons, as they look for future leaders. They do have to do that, but where do you think future leaders start? And what about the future managers and experts? Everyone comes in at the ground level at some point and they all need inspirational managers to help them progress.

So, get on board with this one and enjoy it because you will feel really proud to see your people progress. When David Roberts won an award at Badenoch & Clark after a challenging time of personal development, his manager, Charlotte Butterfield, gave the loudest cheer because she was so delighted with his achievement. The benefits of being known as an exceptional talent manager will far outweigh your impact on your own workload – a high-performing team will deliver much better results than you could ever achieve on your own.

Build your manager network

It is impossible to help people to manage their careers if you don't know what the options/possibilities are in the business. A great network will always stand you in good stead, not just because it will help you spot opportunities for your people but also because it will help you be a more effective organisational manager as well as a team manager.

❝ It is impossible to help people ... if you don't know what the options/possibilities are. ❞

It does require you to be a bit sociable, but if that is really hard for you, either because you are reserved or under real pressure, then feel free to cheat. Identify one person who is a really good networker and build that relationship, then, if they are willing, you can piggyback on their contacts. However, don't do this as the easy option because it is always most effective to have your own network. To build a network:

▶ go out for lunch or a drink with the managers in your peer team to chat about work, share information, discuss problems and find out what is happening in their own teams

▶ link to your internal customers to understand how you can serve them better and build useful relationships as you go

▶ get to know other people at conferences or training events, bring peer teams together to share learning or set up a social event for managers at your level from across the organisation.

Action

All these ideas will pay off, as long as you use them. It is perfectly possible to go to a meeting with network potential and just talk to the people you already know, so always allow some time for preparation:

▶ Before going to any network meeting, think about your people, their challenges, talents and aspirations. Keep these in the back of your mind as you chat.

▶ Keep looking for the project or job that will stretch your high-potential people. For others who are already maximising their talents, listen out for opportunities that they might enjoy – this might be joining the social committee or going on a jolly to schmooze a customer.

▶ If you need a particular person for your team or a specific piece of work, let people know across the network. Even if your organisation requires a full recruitment process for each job, this will still make sure that talented people know about the opportunities.

▶ When your team members come up with good ideas that will also benefit others, use your network to make sure that they get through to the right people. There's nothing more demoralising than a great idea hitting the dust for want of trying. It also helps you build the profile of your people.

Ideas for personal development

Personal development is so much more than just promotion, so it is useful to start thinking in a different way about the possibilities. Oliver Hickson, at COI, has used the following options with his team.

▶ Obviously, promotion from within.

▶ Secondment to specialist areas in the organisation – great for giving someone a wider view of the work and providing a stimulating new experience without moving levels.

▶ Sitting in the client's business for two weeks to six months. This builds understanding of the client's needs while also providing experience of another working environment. Of course, there is a risk that they will be poached, but it is worth taking. At worst you would end up with advocates in the client's office! ➤

> ▶ Take a sabbatical or career break. Increasingly, organisations are offering this option and it allows people to travel, write a book or just have more time with the family. Oliver always talks it through with the team to make sure that they all agree, they will have to pick up the slack, but at least they know that they can have their time if they want it.

Once you start thinking about it, I'm sure you will come up with equally interesting opportunities. It is all about being creative, just like Della Garmory, at Nationwide, was when she had to turn Lisa down after an excellent interview:

> For a number of reasons I just couldn't give her the job, even though she had clearly outgrown her present management role and there was a risk we'd lose her. Then I realised that I had a person in my team who had outgrown the consultant job and needed to develop management skills, so I got this idea for a swap.

> I spoke to Bob, Lisa's boss, and suggested that I pay Carol's salary for her to do Lisa's job and he paid Lisa's salary for her to come and do Carol's job. He thought it was a brilliant idea – it gave him nothing to lose and everything to gain.

> Lisa picked up the job superbly and really developed. The secondment for Carol didn't work out in the end, but I found another six-month secondment for her somewhere else in the business, which then became open-ended. So Lisa applied for Carol's job and got it! We've been working together now for three years and she's fantastic. It was a real moment in terms of being creative – we just took grade and status out of it and did the best for the people, which also turned out to be best for the business.

Expect the best

Just letting people know that they have talent and setting up a development plan for them may not be enough. Those concerned don't always see what you see, so you may have to raise the level of urgency and 'hold their toes to the fire' until they get it. This is about balancing the support and challenge. Make clear your belief in their ability and that you expect high-quality from them, then provide challenges that really stretch them. However, be sure to always back it up with the support they need.

Committed people will work really hard for a manager who listens when needed, gives the right information and tools for the job and makes a real fuss when it goes well.

❝ Raise the level of urgency and 'hold their toes to the fire'. ❞

There is one consequence of this – you have to expect that mistakes will be made and not lose your rag and fell into blame. Any hint that you are risk-averse and people will watch their backs, which is totally contradictory to personal development. So, with any mistake, listen first to make sure that you understand what happened, talk through the learning for the future and work with them to put it right. Handle this well and you will build huge levels of trust and credibility that will increase loyalty and mean that people really want to give of their best.

Action

▶ Identify a piece of work that you can delegate. Choose the person who will benefit most from the opportunity, help them to understand the task and provide clear objectives and timelines with regular check-in points.

▶ Make time to talk about how it is going. Share with the team who is doing what, so you can celebrate significant milestones.

▶ If there is a lack of action, it might be a step too far or due to lack of confidence. Alternatively, you may be looking over their shoulder a bit too much. Either way, do what is necessary to support that person in moving forward.

▶ If someone is really struggling, be prepared to let them move back or sideways. Being clear from the outset that this is a possibility can be reassuring and a real spur for those who are determined never to let it happen!

▶ Never back away from telling the truth. If someone is dive-bombing on a challenge, tell them. Give clear and specific feedback so that the person understands the problem, find out what will help them to move forward – more training, coaching or information – then agree new deadlines.

Look beyond the first impression

Ben Wood, at Mace, talks about Mark Lee as one of his success stories.

When Mark came to work with the team, he didn't have a great record and now he's the most sought-after planner within Mace – he's absolutely fantastic! The guy can produce great diagrams of how something is going to be built and explain it to people who don't understand building at all.

To begin with he was shy about coming forward. I think he'd had problems within Mace, so I did all I could to encourage him to do his best work. As a result, we worked together really well. Whenever there was a problem, we'd get in the next day for 7.30 a.m., get the drawings out, replan it and come up with a master plan. Then we would argue about who came up with the idea in the first place! Mark would take the bit of paper away and return with a presentation to pin on the wall and you'd think, 'Cor! That's a good idea!'

Now if the boss has any planning problems, he's on the phone to 'borrow Mark for this job we've a problem with'. It's one of the delights of management to see someone come through like that. I used to like getting praise for myself, but it's much more satisfying when people say that your team are working well. If you have got a team that are performing, it's great.

Celebrate success

Building talent is hard work for everyone, so make sure to have a good time when it goes well. Congratulations and fun is also a wonderful way to reinforce desired behaviour and demonstrate that you value people, so they are more likely to work hard in the future.

❝ Congratulations and fun ... demonstrate that you value people, so they are more likely to work hard in the future. ❞

But it is not just successes that need to be valued. Some of the best ideas in business have come about as a result of mistakes and they are certainly the source of some of the best learning, so don't just deal with them in a darkened room. If you are really canny, you will celebrate them, too. Alan

Bishop, at COI, talks about enjoying the 'thoughtful mistakes and glorious attempts – you can't condemn them when they come from the right attitude'.

Action

▶ When you allocate a piece of work, set clear objectives and deadlines along the way so that you can celebrate small achievements as well as the big events.

▶ Remember to include support staff – they are often left out when it comes to partying with the high-flyers.

▶ Make sure that the style of celebration fits the person. Quiet types won't thank you for razzmatazz in front of the whole office – offering to pay for them to take their partners out for a quiet dinner or just a thank you note would probably go down better. So think carefully before you act.

▶ Don't forget yourself. If one of your team is successful, it is because you have done a good job of managing the process, so join in the fun and enjoy your joint achievement.

How will I fit it all in?

It does sound like a lot, I agree. However, this is high-priority work – after all, it is people who will ensure that your organisation grows and flourishes. Without them working well in their present jobs and without you making sure that there is a supply of talent coming through, the business will falter.

❝It is people who will ensure that your organisation grows and flourishes. ❞

The most important thing is to recognise that talent development, with its tough and joyful times, is in the job description of every manager and comes high on the list for an inspirational manager. Even if management is only part of your remit, you can't afford to ignore it. So, if the pressure really is too much, then talk with your manager about how to reorganise your time.

Fran Rodgers, at Northampton Borough Council, has an exceptionally difficult job helping to turn around a struggling organisation. The pressure is on every day, with no let-up, yet she still manages to think about talent management.

> We take more risks because of our situation – stretching people whether they feel ready or not – so we also have to plan for when it's a step too far. An old manager of mine used to say "give a busy person a job". I didn't thank her for it at the time, but in many ways it's true. I just have to look at each task and ask who in the team can do it and let them have a go.

Madeline, who works in Fran's team, used to feel really down about the situation. Since Fran arrived, the pressure has been at least as bad, but the support levels have risen considerably. Recently she smiled at the end of the day and said, 'I'm pleased with my work today and I'm really proud of what I've achieved.' So, keeping up the pressure, but in a supportive way, has helped Madeline find a new and more satisfying way of working.

Fran sees her role as that of being an anchor, underpinning everyone so they can get on with their work. While she is always busy, she will take five minutes to support anyone who needs it. If she can do it in those exceptionally tough circumstances, my guess is that you can have a go, too.

Action

Arrange to speak to your manager if you are having difficulty finding the time for talent management:

▶ Make a list of your present objectives and associated tasks to take with you. Doing a time management log for a couple of days will help you form an accurate picture of how you use time and highlight inappropriate interruptions or calls on your day.

▶ If your manager doesn't see the value of developing people, then find a mentor elsewhere in the organisation who is known to be good at this work. You may also speak to them about your own career development, because your manager will not give time to it.

▶ If your manager agrees on the importance of this work, look through the list of demands on your time and agree where the priorities lie. You may be able to hand some of the work on to your peers, work smarter or maybe some of the work can be delayed. It is always a matter of prioritising because if you really want to do something, you will find a way.

Expect your stars to leave you

If you are an excellent talent manager, people will come to you to develop their careers. The downside is that they will move on, leaving you back at the beginning with new people in your team. It is a double-edged sword!

Paul Dunmore, at Thomson Directories, has to deal with this all the time. When I met him, he had just lost Adam, his star man.

I work with him to get promotion and then I lose out, but I have to be open-minded about it. Some managers will be discouraging because they don't want to lose the person, but that's really short-sighted. In the time Adam worked with me, I got better value for money than if he'd seen this as a dead-end job with nothing to aim for, no goals.

There was another guy, Mark, who is now trainer for the Northern region. When he came to me, he was unsuccessful, so I set out to discover what made him tick. I found that he wanted satisfaction, acclaim and having people look up to him, which explained his ambition to be a trainer. So I put it to him, 'If you apply to the training department right now, they'll laugh at you because your results are so poor. You need to show them how good you are, that you are top of the tree, that your sales figures are exemplary, otherwise why would they want you to train other people?'

We worked together until his figures went from rubbish to an A grade and he achieved his dream. It was disappointing when he went because I lost his figures and his positive influence on the team, but now I can use that as a success story with the people who work with me – you tell me what you want and I'll help you get there. What an inspiration that is!

Lack of opportunity in the organisation

There may well come a time when the organisation doesn't have the right opportunities for your stars, which is really tough. This is particularly significant if you are in a small or flat organisation in which case there may well be nowhere for people to progress. Yet if you still want the best people in your team, you will have to spend time developing their potential, so don't be put off.

Whatever you do, they will eventually go. High-performing people will always be looking for the next step, either because they are ambitious or just because they love to learn and develop. So you have two choices: you can pretend that development is not important and just get on with the day to day, in which case they will leave out of frustration. Or you can make it clear that you will help them to build their careers and you realise this means they will leave, in fact you will encourage it! It is hard, but it is still the best way forward. Better to have great people for a while than to settle for 'good enough' and lose them anyway. The positive spin-off is that you get a reputation for being a great place to develop and other stars will seek you out.

> **❝ Better to have great people for a while than to settle for 'good enough' and lose them anyway. ❞**

Summary

▶ Being a great talent manager means the best people will want to work for you, so it is well worth the effort.

▶ Develop your talent-spotting muscle. Look beyond the obvious for what lies beneath.

▶ Understand that some people want promotion, but others want to stay where they are and do great work. Both ends of the spectrum need your attention.

▶ Build a strong network of your peers, so that you get to know about opportunities for your people as they arise

▶ Be tough and only settle for the best a person can do, even if they don't yet see how good they are. With your support, challenge and encouragement, the sky's the limit.

▶ Celebrate at every opportunity – it will make it all worthwhile and inspire the next round of activity. Include 'glorious attempts' and honest mistakes for the learning value that they bring.

▶ If you don't have time with your present workload, do some reorganising because this is too important to leave out.

▶ Expect people to leave you and move on. It is a sign of your success and something that you can feel really proud of. It will have an impact on the team's results, of course, but will also ensure that other good people beat a path to your door.

Action plan
Today

▶ Set dates in your diary for career discussions, including a meeting with your own manager. Set aside time next week to plan the process.

Next week

▶ Plan meetings with your people. Be clear in your own mind who you think can move on and who needs to stay where they are. Check that you are not just trying to hold on to good people! Gather feedback about their work, consider what you think their talents are and what you would suggest for their next steps. Make a list of the questions you want to ask and the areas you need to explore.

▶ Tell the team about your plans in the next meeting. Give them time to ask questions. If this is new to you all, be prepared for some concerns about an underlying agenda. Be as reassuring as you can and accept that they may need to experience it before they believe you.

▶ If you need support, ask for a mentor or look for a colleague who is really good at this and find out how they do it.

Next month

▶ Work your way through the one-to-one meetings. Meet with your mentor or colleagues to debrief and see what you could have done differently.

▶ Find one thing each week to celebrate. It doesn't have to be big – just a team 'thank you' or a visit to the pub after work is fine. It demonstrates that you really mean what you say and it is worth them getting involved.

▶ Look at the organisation's strategy and decide what talents you need to develop for the future.

▶ Meet up with peers whenever you can to find out what the options are in the business. You are looking for new projects, promotions, additional roles (social committee and so on), job swaps ... anything that will stretch your people's thinking and understanding.

CHAPTER

11

Holding the tough conversations

'Admit when you are wrong and ask for help when you need it.'

Charlotte Butterfield, Badenoch & Clark

Inspirational managers never leave tough conversations to fester in the background because they realise that problems ignored grow to gargantuan proportions. Allowing people to deliver inadequate work is not an option, as it shows little respect and provides no appropriate challenge. This level of honesty lies at the heart of inspirational management and getting to grips with it will earn you credibility, respect and piece of mind.

❝ Problems ignored grow to gargantuan proportions. ❞

The fundamental question is, do you see your job as just delivering work on time or delivering on time in a way that also makes the best of your people? Focusing on the former will tempt you to:

▶ feel frustrated if the work is not done in a timely manner or as well as you expected

▶ take over and deliver the final product yourself because time is short

▶ back off explaining what the problem is because handling the fallout will take time away from the next piece of work to be delivered.

This has 'self-fulfilling prophecy' written all over it: 'If you deliver work to me that isn't good enough, I will take over and do it for you, so you don't learn how to do it better next time, which means I have to do it for you ...'

The inspirational way is to see every problem as an opportunity for learning, so people can improve, grow their skills and do their own jobs without the manager taking over. Of course, this means facing up to the different reasons for underperformance:

▶ the person has potential to deliver well once the problem is explained to them and they are given coaching support to improve

▶ the person in the wrong job, but has the right attitude for the organisation, so needs to be moved to a more appropriate role.

▶ the person is just not up to the required standard and has no potential for improvement, so needs to be moved out.

These are tough conversations to have, but speaking out in the early stages will make things much easier. Doing so will also increase the chances of success, reducing the likelihood of having to face the really tough one of moving out a poor performer.

Addressing performance issues

It's all in the relationship

Allison Nicoll, at Freedom Finance, always addresses poor performance as early as she can:

> I set out to help them recognise the drop in standard themselves. The best way is to point out that their performance has been fantastic in the past and saying, 'Gosh, you did so well there, how come you have gone downhill so fast? After all, we know you can do it.' I think when someone is underperforming they get stuck with the idea that they can't do it and will never have good times again, so reinforcing their past success gives them confidence.

To achieve this, Allison puts a lot of effort into staying up to date with her people. If she thinks that there is a problem, she will take them out to the local coffee shop or, if they smoke, go outside with them while they have a cigarette. 'When it's on their own terms they will be more comfortable talking about the problem and, if they need to have a cry, they can cry outside without having to be with everyone else.'

Many performance issues are co-created with managers who won't face the truth. Inspirational managers never wait in the hope that standards will improve. Instead, they talk about it immediately and look for ways to help the person develop. Like Stacey Mitchell who meets with Tesh Kataria regularly to look at the figures. If it is not going well, they talk it through and look for actions that will turn it around. Charlotte Butterfield meets her consultants each week to find out how things are going. Because the meetings are frequent, people feel free to speak up when something is not going well, so action can be taken to address it.

❝ Many performance issues are co-created with managers who won't face the truth. ❞

Delivering a tough message

If all your efforts to help the person improve have not made a difference or they are is not taking your concern seriously enough, then it is time to address the issue. How easy this is will depend on the levels of trust in your team.

If the relationships are good, their trust will be high and you can be more direct. Paul Dunmore, at Thomson Directories, talks about a time when the whole team was underperforming. He had been away running a course for the company and they had taken their foot off the gas. He talked with them about it straight away and told them very clearly how disappointed he was. He was tough and didn't pull his punches, but he did it with respect, so it was over with quickly. 'They were on fire afterwards. They felt a bit guilty as well as knowing it wasn't a good job.'

If you don't have strong relationships, then it is more difficult. As an inspirational manager you will be working to improve trust levels in your team and, contrary to popular opinion, dealing with your difficult issues might be exactly the right way to do it. High performers will always know when another person isn't up to the job, not least because they will be picking up the slack. If you don't deal with this, it will cost you in respect and, eventually, they will lose heart or look for a better manager. When you do deal with it, you will go up in their estimation and the bar will be raised for the whole team.

❝ When you do deal with it, you will go up in their estimation and the bar will be raised for the whole team. ❞

There are several stages to the process of delivering a tough message:

- preparing the ground
- planning the meeting
- telling the truth
- follow-up meetings and planning.

Preparing the ground

There are specific procedures that you need to follow from the moment you are concerned about performance. If you are not clear what these are, talk with your HR representative and find out, because the sooner you embark on this process, the easier it will be. When Gill Crowther was Head of Great Managers at Microsoft she always encouraged them to 'think formally from the moment there is a gap in performance. This doesn't mean you don't believe the person can improve, but does mean it won't take years to move them on if they can't.'

Most importantly, from the outset the person must understand clearly:

- what good looks like and exactly what they need to do to deliver
- the concerns you have – with specific feedback on work to date and objectives for moving forward
- what they need to do to improve – clear outputs, timelines and measures
- how they can get the support they need – from you, an appropriate colleague, coach or mentor
- how they are progressing – whether or not the work they are putting in is sufficient to make the difference.

Given that this whole process will provoke anxiety, it is important to make sure that they have really taken in what you are saying. If you feel that there is hope, tell them that and make it clear that you are willing to give the support they need – any encouragement will improve the chances of success. However, it is important not to give false hope. People need to know when the risks are high so that they can respond accordingly.

Action

▶ Always hold performance conversations in a place where you won't be interrupted as this can confuse the issue.

▶ Make sure that you have been totally clear by asking the person to summarise the discussion at the end of the meeting, then clarify any misunderstandings.

▶ Follow up with an e-mail, not only to help them take in the seriousness of the situation, but to provide the formal, written element of the process, should you need it.

Planning the meeting

If you follow this process and are clear enough in what you tell the person, you may find that the standard improves. However, if the work continues to be below par, you will have to give a formal warning. Inspirational managers plan this sort of conversation really carefully, knowing that it is not going to be easy for anyone.

Action

▶ Look back over the records from your performance discussions so far and summarise all the steps that have been taken to help them progress.

▶ Look for aspects of their work that is going well or better than it was. If you think the person has the potential to improve, this will inspire them and demonstrate that you want them to succeed.

▶ Think about the person – what are they like and how do you think they will react to your decision? If they are generally quite robust, you may be able to be more straightforward, but if you think they are more fragile, think carefully about how you speak.

▶ Think about how you feel going into this meeting. Do you feel defensive? If so, focus on what you need so that you can go into the meeting feeling more open to the person involved.

▶ If being sensitive to other people isn't one of your strengths, seek out colleagues who are good at it and find out how they would handle it or go to HR and get some coaching.

Telling the truth

Set an appropriate time and place for the meeting and take the person through the main points, as you have planned.

- *State the case* – speak clearly about the issue that needs to be addressed, outlining your concerns.

- *Understand* – listen carefully to what the person has to say, asking questions to make sure that you fully understand their perspective. There may be more to it than you had realised.

- *Provide encouragement* – if any area of their work has gone well, recognise the efforts made. You want to inspire them to improved performance, but take care not to use this as a way to make yourself feel better or there is a risk the praise will overshadow the true message.

- *Look for the learning* – discuss the different elements and look for the learning that can be taken on both sides. If relevant, put it into the context of any development work done to date.

- *Agree the next steps* – ask the person how they might improve. If they can come up with ideas themselves, it will be more powerful. Make clear that you have objectives, timescales and measures that need to be met. Agree to revisit this when they have had time to settle and think it through.

- *Provide good reasons for changing* – make clear how they will benefit from making a real effort to improve.

- *Implications of not improving* – make sure they understand what will happen if they don't deliver as discussed.

- *Follow-up* – send an e-mail summary of the discussion to ensure that there is clear understanding on both sides.

Tesh Kataria, at Tower Homes, has learned that a willingness to listen early on in the discussion is extremely important. He has tried going straight to exploring why the problem occurred and looking for the learning, but found that it really didn't work. People want to justify themselves and defend their choices – it is a natural instinct to show why it isn't their fault, so listen well and assess how valid the reasoning is.

It is really important to keep your head. Charlotte Butterfield, at Badenoch & Clark, talks about the need for an inspirational manager to 'keep the ego in check', whether in times of success or difficulties. Focus on your own needs so that you can do your best, but never forget that the other person will be feeling even worse than you do.

❝ It is really important to keep your head. ❞

When problems have occurred with your team you will have played your part in that, so be prepared to own up to what you could have done differently. Apart from anything else, providing a role model for taking responsibility is really positive.

You need four clear outputs from a performance conversation:

▶ immediate actions – either crisis management or longer-term change

▶ clear understanding of the problem and how it has occurred

▶ agreement about how to ensure that change happens

▶ what *you* could have done differently to support them in delivering a positive outcome.

Andrew Rothesay, at Boehringer Ingelheim, recommends that you 'always stick to the facts – be honest about what is working and what isn't, being clear that this isn't personal, it is about business. But you must accept some will feel it personally, so always be compassionate.'

A first meeting may only deliver a rescue plan, because the discussion will raise all sorts of feelings, such as shock, upset, even embarrassment, especially if you have let underperformance ride in the past. So be compassionate and don't go in all guns blazing. Instead take the approach that mistakes happen, so you both need to learn from it and move on. However, as an inspirational manager, it is really important not to back off the clear message that this level of performance/behaviour is not acceptable and that carrying on as before is not an option.

Follow the meeting up with a written summary of the discussion and the agreed next steps. Usually an e-mail will do, but confirm this with your HR department.

A good relationship always helps

'He's a bit like my dad sometimes – he knows from the tone of my voice when I'm down and he'll always ask what's up.' This is how Katherine speaks about being managed by Paul Dunmore, at Thomson Directories.

A while ago, she was missing her targets, which she knew would also mean Paul missed his. 'When we underperform it means he loses out, too, but he'll never mention it. Instead, he looks to see how he can help us get back on track.'

Paul will always give warning of the content of a difficult meeting to allow the person time to think it through and prepare. As a result, when he sat down with Katherine, they were already on the same wavelength:

> Katherine had already said that she was disappointed with her results, so we started off with that.
>
> We talked about why that was and what she was finding difficult.
>
> I reassured her that she has the ability to do the job, even though present results weren't good enough. I talked about her ambition, pointing out that I want her to be an obvious choice for the next management job. I said to her, 'You've worked so hard to get here, we have to make sure you are in a position to grasp the opportunities when they arise.'
>
> Then we considered our relationship – did we communicate enough when she was struggling, could I have done more, was she hiding away from me? And if she was, how could I make sure it doesn't happen again. At the first inkling of something going wrong, she needs to talk with me so she doesn't start to go backwards.

As you can see, it was a tough one for Katherine. She knows that she's good, but she also knew that she hadn't been delivering as well as expected. The whole conversation was made a great deal easier by the relationship she has with Paul. She knows that he is committed to her success and has faith in her ability to do the job really well. Not only that, but he is keen to see her be a manager in her own right.

The key factors to note are that:

▶ Katherine knew that there was a problem – there were no surprises

- she knew that Paul believed in her ability to do the work and wanted to see her move on to the next stage of her career

- he got her to identify the problem first, so she stated her own bad news

- they worked at it as a team and Paul took his responsibility for the problem.

Follow-up meetings and planning

Book a follow-up meeting within a couple of days of your tough conversation. People need time to come to terms with negative comments, but not so much time that they start to stew. What you are looking for is to stem the tide of poor outputs and get the person back to productive work as soon as possible. There is nothing worse than having them sit on worries for a long time because it is all-consuming and even more distraction from their work.

Get the person back to productive work as soon as possible.

The follow-up meeting needs to:

- *Revisit the original discussion* – give the person time to talk about their reactions and how they feel

- *Recap on the relationship* – talk through how you both allowed the situation to get out of hand

- *Emphasise a positive attitude* – encourage them not to lay blame but focus on action and change

- *Clarify what needs to happen* – reiterate what you each need to do to ensure that it doesn't happen again

- *Create an action plan* – confirm any plans from the first meeting and build them into a robust action plan, including clear objectives, deadlines and measurable outputs.

If the person goes away feeling that they have learned something and eager to get back to work and deliver, then you have done an excellent job. But remember not to stop there. If you want to avoid being back here again in a couple of months, you need to put regular meetings in place. Go for more frequent one-to-ones at the outset to ensure that you give them as much support as you can. If necessary, meet each week or every couple of days, depending on the issue. As soon as you see improvement, you can extend the time between meetings.

Always keep the promises you make in performance meetings. No one fails alone – the manager is always part of the equation. Poor results, shocks and difficulties with customers or suppliers are all shortcomings of both manager and report. Not a happy thought, but as soon as you take responsibility at least you can begin to create change, which is far more comfortable than feeling you are constantly on the back foot.

❝ No one fails alone – the manager is always part of the equation. ❞

The final call

Most managers have had to terminate employment for poor performance at some point in their careers. This is a conversation that no one wants to have as it makes a major impact on the person's life, leading to all manner of changes and implications. No wonder the list of excuses for not doing it is a mile long.

It is a terrible feeling to tell someone that they are no good at a job, even though your careful performance management should mean it is no surprise. You will probably find that you lose sleep, feel anxious and become totally preoccupied. There is one school of thought that says the right person to give the news is the one who feels most distressed by it. At least then, they will apply compassion and work for the best possible outcome.

Tough as it is, inspirational managers always bite the bullet. They realise that if they don't, there are real risks to the business, both in terms of poor results and impact on other people. They also recognise that when someone is not performing, somewhere in their heart they know it and everyone around them certainly knows it, so it will be a real relief when action is finally taken.

To achieve the best outcome for the organisation and the person concerned, there are some obvious steps to follow:

- be clear about your decision
- find out about the legalities
- plan the process
- tell the truth.

Be clear about your decision

It is very easy to get caught up with the personal impact. You do need to think of this, but it should not be your first port of call. There are several things that come before that.

- First consider the business – will keeping this person in post have a negative impact or stop the team moving forward effectively?
- If the answer is 'Yes', then think about whether or not there is another place in the organisation where the person could utilise their strengths. If so, see if you can arrange for that to happen.
- If that won't work, then you have to terminate employment. If you don't, you will make life difficult for everyone, not only the underperformer. You can't let one person put the business and other people at risk.

Because it is such a hard decision, arrange for some time with your own boss to talk through how you feel about it, what help you need in order to carry it through and how to arrange the best financial deal you can. Because once the decision is made, as an inspirational manager, your aim is to help that person walk out of the door with their head held high and self-esteem intact.

Everyone has the capacity to be a star somewhere if they are prepared to make the effort, so failing in this job doesn't make that person a failure. There is an important point that many people fail to grasp or deride as a whitewash. You do people no favours by letting them continue in work that doesn't suit them. Instead, help them move on to something that they can enjoy and be wildly successful at.

Keep the context in mind

Nothing will take away the pain of what you have to do, but it may help to remember that settling for second best serves no one. I recall working with a manager who went through hell before telling someone to go. The impact at the time was devastating and it took the manager ages to recover, never mind the person concerned. However, when they accidentally met in a bar six months later, the ex-employee thanked his ex-manager. He knew he would have carried on doing the work he hated, and even though he still didn't have a new job, he felt better than he had done for a very long time.

Think about a time when you were doing a job badly. My guess is that you didn't enjoy it and felt pretty miserable. I certainly was when doing a job that didn't play to my strengths – it is a desperate experience. As soon as I moved to something I enjoyed and had a talent for, life looked up and I was a different person. It will be the same for anyone in the wrong place. Unless we can use our talents, we are always holding back and the long-term effects can be very negative.

As an inspirational manager, you have to do the right thing – to take the actions and decisions that will give the best outcome for the most people in the long run. Short-term fixes will always cause more harm than good. So, leaving a person to languish in the wrong job is bad for them and everyone who works with them, because they will be picking up the slack and building a huge backlog of resentment. So it is your job as manager to look for the right action and move on it as soon as possible because any decision you make impacts on the team, business and individual. You can't look at any of this in isolation.

Find out about the legalities

You may already have spoken to the HR department about your problem. If not, make contact and show them the written documents outlining the process to date. They will help you work out the legal requirements and support you in taking action in the right way. This is critical – it will cost you considerable time in tribunals if you don't follow the correct procedures.

There are two main concerns for an inspirational manager:

▶ that this discussion should never be a shock – an inspirational manager never starts a disciplinary process without all the procedures in place: that is, the direct report will have a clear understanding of the problem, have been given the chance to improve and had ample warning that the standard of work was still cause for concern

▶ to take full responsibility for managing the task well – they will never expect HR or anyone else to do it for them. This is their relationship, so they want to do the very best they can for their direct report, however hard it is.

Plan the process

Even though the person wasn't right for the job, as an inspirational manager you will want them to walk away with their self-esteem as high as possible under the circumstances. To achieve this:

▶ put yourself in the other person's shoes and think about the best way for them to hear this news.

▶ consider whether it will be helpful for the person to speak to someone who is not involved, so that they can be honest about how they feel

▶ arrange for the person to leave the building in a private way if they want to

▶ consider what you will say to the team members and when will be the best time to tell them

▶ think about what you will need once it is completed – a bit of support may not go amiss!

Tell the truth

Helena Moore, at Bromford Housing Group, goes for preserving as much dignity as possible. She advocates the following approach.

▶ Tell the person the truth without mincing your words, then give them time to recover and take in what has been said.

▶ Discuss the circumstances in as transparent, clear and direct a way as possible. It is really important that they understand fully why what is happening. Give as much time as you can to this.

▶ Get the person some support. As manager you are probably not the right person to do this, so, if possible, sort out some counselling or refer them to your Employee Assistance Programme (EAP).

▶ Consider career counselling or look at alternative jobs with the person, if they are willing. This will help the individual understand where their strengths lie and look for a more appropriate job where they can thrive.

▶ Let the person choose how to leave. Some want to say goodbye – psychologically it makes it easier to finish and move on. However, others prefer to go away quietly because they don't feel comfortable seeing other colleagues or they may feel upset, ashamed or embarrassed at what has happened.

A really important part of this is a discussion about the person's strengths and possible next jobs. Not only does this help them to think about another workplace in a positive way, but also makes it clear that they are is not a failure in themselves, they just weren't right for this job. That the manager recognises this and is willing to take the time to discuss it is a real affirmation to go away with and can be a considerable help in the healing process.

Handling the conversation in a way that can help the person move forward to the next step doesn't take away the distress of having 'messed up' another person's life, but it will help you to feel that you have done the best you can and that is all you can do in the circumstances.

Summary

▶ Telling the tough truth isn't comfortable, but neither is avoidance. The former is better for the business and everyone involved.

▶ It is always easier to sort out problems in the context of a good relationship. If you meet regularly to discuss performance, there will be no surprises and you can work things out together.

▶ When things are not right, speak out as soon as you can: ➤

- prepare well – never have this conversation 'on the hoof'
- take time in the meeting to discuss the issues fully
- agree what actions need to be taken and follow this up with a written summary
- agree follow-up meetings to track progress and ensure that the changes are being made.

▶ Telling someone that they have to go is extremely hard, but it is worse for everyone if you put it off.

▶ Get backup from your HR department to make sure you are following the correct disciplinary processes, but never expect them to do it for you.

▶ To make the decision, consider the business first, then look for the best way to tell that particular person.

Action plan

Today

▶ Consider the people in your team. Are they all doing well enough in their jobs?

▶ If not, then be honest with yourself about the next steps that you have been avoiding. Prioritise and see which need to be addressed first.

▶ Decide which you are going to act on.

Next week

▶ Arrange a meeting with your underperformer and prepare for the meeting.

▶ If you have someone whom you believe needs to be moved out of the business, write down your reasons for this action, taking into consideration how much effort you have made to help the person progress or improve their performance and how clearly you have shared your concerns.

▶ Talk with your own manager and get backing for your decision.

Next month

▶ Talk with HR to find out about the formal side of the process.

- Identify an inspirational manager in your organisation who handles these discussions well and ask for a coaching session.
- Hold your first performance management meeting and set follow-up meetings in your diary.
- Talk with HR about provisions for the person you need to move out. Do all you can to get the very best deal. Find out about counselling support or the Employee Assistance Programme (EAP).
- Choose a time that makes sense. Maybe a Friday, if you think that the person will need time away or else a week day if you think they will need to talk it through again quickly.
- Hold the meeting, allowing as much time as the person needs. Give them information about the deal and back-up support, then leave time for them to think it through.
- Be available if the person needs to speak to you.
- Get yourself some support, too – this won't have been easy!

Recruiting the best

'Sit back and weigh things up, regardless of the demands on your time.'

Pam Nock, Northampton Borough Council

For Helena Moore, at Bromford Housing Group, the biggest mistake she ever made was to take on someone she wasn't sure of. Now she would 'rather leave an empty space than take on the wrong person'. Inspirational managers recognise the importance only not of skill, but of personality and fit with the team, so they won't take on someone unless they are really sure.

My colleague, Gill Crowther, ex Head of Great Managers at Microsoft, talks about 'closing the loop'. You can have a fantastic performance management process that enables you to manage well and develop talent, but if you don't bring in the right people to begin with, your job is just that much harder. Yet, in reality, managers can easily panic when they are under-staffed, going for just anyone rather than have empty seats. This short-term thinking creates a vicious cycle, because the wrong people either won't stay or you will have to ask them to leave and then you are back to needing more recruits. If you want the best results, you have to get the best people on board.

How to recruit the best

There are several stages to the recruiting process and all are significant. If you want to ensure that you get the people who will complement and add to your team, don't skimp on time.

Understand your needs

Make sure that you are clear about what you need for the team. You will need to consider two key factors:

▶ the attitude required to suit the team and demonstrate the agreed behaviour

▶ the skills needed to ensure delivery of the required outputs.

As an inspirational manager, you will realise that this is the right order – attitude first, skill set second. You can have the most able specialists possible, but if they don't fit the ethos of your team, it will never be quite right. Better the right attitude with a bit less experience – a miserable expert won't do their best work.

❝Attitude first, skill set second. ❞

Action

▶ Look at the people already in your team and clarify the style and attitude that will enable a new person to fit in and get on with the work.

▶ Revisit the organisational values and behaviour in your team charter to help you define the person you need.

▶ Consider the specific task and identify the attributes required, such as the ability to build relationships across the organisation or with customers.

Draw up a brief taking all these factors into account. Be as specific as possible as a means of gaining the support you need from HR and reduce the risk of looking only at skills during the interview.

What about diversity?

Isn't there a risk that you will lose out on diversity? Surely that wouldn't be good for the team or the business, never mind being illegal.

Let's make a distinction here. You want people who hold similar values and attitudes to life, but who they are in terms of age, sexual preference, ethnicity, gender, learning style etc is not relevant. In fact, the more varied the life experience, the more the person is likely to bring to the team. If you are looking for a trustworthy person or a good communicator, you need to concentrate on that attribute and all sorts of people share those.

At Freedom Finance, they are very clear about the people they want, those who are approachable, friendly, helpful and team players. No limit there then!

Prepare the ground

The recruitment process is the first contact applicants have with the organisation, so you want them to get a feel of what it will be like to work with you. The inspirational manager wants them to feel really excited and determined to get the job or be clear that this isn't the job for them – both these reactions will really help you. To achieve this, think about the design of the advert, the style of interview, who will do the interviewing and how they can convey the 'feel' of the business and the team.

Action

Consider the following.

▶ Do you want people who have done similar work or people with different experience and skills?

▶ Is there a way to advertise internally or talk with HR about a waiting list of people who have already contacted the organisation because they want to work there?

▶ Who do you need on the interview panel? You must be there so that you can gauge whether or not the interviewee will suit the team, but you may also want a technical expert and someone who can give an independent view to make sure that you don't just recruit people in your own likeness.

▶ What style of interview do you want? Is an assessment centre appropriate, do you want the promising candidates to spend time in the team, will you include your boss? Get dates in the diaries of relevant people and make clear exactly what it is you need from them.

▶ What information do you need from applicants prior to interview? So that you can weed out unsuitable people from the outset.

▶ How can you show the interviewee what the job is actually like, so that they can make an informed choice?

The process needs to attract the right people and put off those who aren't suitable. The clearer you are at the outset, the more time you will have for potential team members and the less you subject other people to a tough interview process when there is no hope.

❝ Attract the right people and put off those who aren't suitable. ❞

The interview process

The more time you give to the interview, the better results you will get. However, if you are under pressure, it will be very tempting to take people on first look. Getting this right requires a change in attitude. This isn't a chore, it is an investment in:

▶ the high performance of your team

▶ your reputation as a manager

▶ the talent pipeline of the organisation.

The flipside is the cost when you get it wrong – even more time interviewing, poor internal and external customer service, never mind the drain on the team when a colleague isn't up to the job. All these scenarios take time one way or another, so investing up front could make all the difference and create a settled team in the long term.

By devoting this amount of time to the process you also show that you are serious about your people and won't just take anyone. This is what high performers are looking for – they don't want the easy option, but they do want to know that they will be taken seriously and will have help in developing their careers. Getting a job in your organisation should create a sense of pride, not just the feeling that they were the best of a bad bunch.

How inspirational managers interview

Let us look at some examples of good technique.

Helena Moore, at Bromford Housing Group

Helena, like other managers at Bromford, uses a bespoke recruitment assessment tool called Open House, designed by Bromford to test candidates against the group's core competencies. It is not about technical skills – these can be tested and explored in other ways. Instead, the purpose of it is to look for:

- aptitude
- attitude
- right fit with the organisation.

Open House gives the opportunity for a wide range of colleagues to get involved in recruitment, which means that they effectively choose their new colleagues, which answers the Bromford desire to be inclusive. The assessment sessions are then complimented with practical tests and interviews.

Fran Rodgers, at Northampton Borough Council

Fran likes to make some additions to the standard local government process of application form and interview to make sure that she doesn't appoint the wrong person. Because Northampton is in such a difficult situation, new employees have to hit the ground running, so Fran must appoint high-calibre people. She wants to understand what their commitment will be to the job and how their experience might fit this situation. With this in mind she:

- Gives them a practical exercise that relates directly to the job – sorting out an in-tray, for example, or a problem that they may have to face. They have 30 minutes to find a solution and then present it back. She wants to know if they can see different options, how well they communicate the issue and solution and how appropriate their solutions are.

- She asks searching questions so they can show what they can do, for example, asking them to talk about a time when they have managed poor performance. She wants to hear how they dealt with the real people, not just a textbook answer. If they don't understand the question, it is a negative sign, although she will always give people another chance in case nerves are taking over.

- Fran is particularly keen to explore their understanding about diversity, because she has found that this separates the 'average' from the 'really good'. For some reason, she finds that people often struggle with this one, so she asks straightforward questions, such as, 'How would you ensure that all sections of the community are consistently getting the right quality of service?' She needs to see that they have thought about it and don't just give the politically correct answer.

▶ She also wants to know if they have prepared for the interview by walking themselves through the job, so, as an icebreaker, she asks what they would do on their first day. In some cases, it has been clear that they don't really know what they have applied for and have no idea what would be involved or what they would need to understand at the outset.

Paul Dunmore, at Thomson Directories

Paul has a very thorough process for recruiting people to his sales team. Applicants go through approximately five interviews and it can take from one to four weeks.

Step 1

Paul conducts a one-to-one interview himself to find out if he likes the person and thinks they will suit the team. During the discussion, he paints a very black picture of the job, telling them just how difficult it is, in an attempt to find out if they are up for the tough times as well as the good.

❝ He paints a very black picture of the job. ❞

Step 2

Those who get through Step 1 are invited to spend time with the team to listen in on calls and hear the knockbacks. 'On the same day, we give them some data cards and get them on the phone to have a go themselves. I listen in from a different room and the team members pay attention, too, because we need to know if they are phone shy. Lucy is a great example – she had little previous experience, but made 230 phone calls in one day. Boy had she got desire!'

Step 3

'If they are still keen, they go on the road with a rep to observe them do five to six appointments and hear what customers say about the company. It also means that they can get information from the horse's mouth and ask those all-important questions: "How long is your working day?', "How much do you earn?", "What's Paul like to work for?", "What happens if you fail … ?" One person went to sleep in the car, so it was the end of the road for him – if he wasn't interested enough to stay awake and learn about the job, then he wasn't the person for this team!'

Step 4

'The applicant does a role-play to sell Thomson Directories to me. This shows me how bright they are and how quickly they pick things up. This job isn't down to qualifications. For example, Adam has just been promoted because he's been in the top three reps for the last three years, but he has no qualifications, no O or A levels. However, he is very streetwise, his dad is the local Arthur Daly and he can sell you anything you want. Adam's brilliant at multi-tasking, he's bright and he'll do it if he thinks it will earn him money.'

Step 5

If Paul is happy with their performance, they meet with Chris Hiles, Paul's boss. This acts as a double-check and provides feedback on whether or not Chris thinks they will fit in with the team.

Nic Larkin, at Data Connection

This company has a very different approach – still time-intensive, but also highly technical. They put a lot of energy and management time into it and all managers are trained to use the same guidelines.

There are two levels of interview. The first interview is enough to admit students who want work over the vacation, while prospective full-time employees go through a second interview. It is extremely tough to get into the company – they recently had 2000 applicants for 20 new roles!

Step 1

Interviewees sit some very difficult technical tests that are marked fairly analytically. There are strict guidelines for marking the tests, with some consideration being given to how applicants express themselves.

Step 2

'First-level interviewers are all managers and the ultimate question is "Do you want this person on your team?" So we mark their technical tests and talk to the person to form a decision.'

Step 3

'The second interview for full-time employees is with a very senior panel of people who assess each person on their communication, what they are like to get on with and, of course, their technical skill. We are looking for the commonsense things, like are they open or defensive, can they express themselves clearly, are they easy to get on with, is this someone you would like to work with?

We're mostly typical techies – very logical, rational thinkers who choose our words carefully. But, because communication is such a central part of our job, it is drummed into everybody right from the start that they have to work as a team. If the interview indicates that someone won't take feedback, making it hard to develop them, then it is unlikely we would take them on. If someone appears to be a complete genius at interview, but is unresponsive, then there is no way we can have them. We just don't have space for people who work all day on their own without talking to anybody.'

The themes of inspirational recruitment

There are some common themes that run through all these examples.

▶ *Know what you are looking for* – Identify the specific behaviour you need to look for in the initial interview and bring in a second opinion. Make sure the interviewees understand the tough aspects of the job so they are really clear what they will be letting themselves in for.

▶ *Focus on attitude* – Make sure the person will fit in with the team and the organisation.

▶ *Meet the team* – Give them some time with a team member and/or the team without you there. It helps them find out more about the reality and ensures the whole team gets involved in the process.

▶ *Meet the boss* – Find out if your boss wants to be involved. You may enjoy having that backup and it will link the interviewee more directly to the organisation.

Giving feedback on the interview

Give feedback as soon as you can. As this is the person's first experience of your organisation, the more respectful and appropriate it is, the more chance there is that they will want to join you. I have known people turn down job offers because they didn't like the way the interview process was handled, so remember that they are interviewing you as well. Speak to them directly, be positive, give them feedback on what you liked and what led you to choose them over others. In short, leave them walking away from that call with a spring in their step and raring to go.

❝ Leave them walking away . . . with a spring in their step. ❞

It is also important not to neglect the people you don't want to employ. Going for interview is a stressful event for most people, so the sooner you let them know the outcome, the better it will be for them. It is also really helpful if you can give some feedback, so that they can learn from the experience and improve their technique or input for the next interview they go to. Of course, you could say, 'Why bother?' – if you don't want the person, why would you spend time giving them feedback to help them get another job? After all, you have got enough on your plate.

The interview process is not just about filling a place, it is also about your image in the sector. This won't be the last interview you ever do and imagine if the word got around that you were really rude and left people hanging without telling them if they had the job. Alternatively, imagine if the person you turned down was so impressed that they set themselves the goal of getting a place on your team? OK, so you don't want them now, but if you give them clear feedback, they may learn from the experience and be just what you need in the future.

The impact of a poor recruitment process

At Freedom Finance, Allison Nicoll learned the hard way about getting the interview process right and handling the new person well at the outset.

One young lady came for a job with us, passed the standard interview and did her training alongside five other new starters. Then we put her into a team that only needed one person. The other four were all on in-bound teams at one end of the office and she was sat right at the other end in a slightly cliquey team she didn't know. They did welcome her, but she didn't have the confidence to make a place for herself, so she eventually shut down and the team just gave up. It was a bit hard, but they felt they'd made an effort without getting a response. It was all very upsetting and eventually we moved her to a different team, but, within three weeks, she left the business.

It went wrong for two reasons:

1 She was the wrong person for our culture. At interview, she came over as very bubbly, outspoken and outgoing, but when she arrived she was like a mouse, so we clearly hadn't found out enough about her personality. We learned a lot from that experience and made a number of changes to our interview process as a result.

2 We didn't take enough care with the first team she worked in. The experience taught us to always put new starters together – even if a team only wanted one person, we would make the sacrifice and put two on it.

As a result, we made some positive changes to our interview process. We now start with a telephone interview to get some basic information and, if they pass that, we bring them in for an assessment day where they:

▶ listen in on calls

▶ do a typing test

▶ take part in a couple of role-plays with the interviewer and a manager

▶ sit with a team member to follow what they do and how they work.

This gives us different perspectives from the interviewer, the manager and team members, which is a real improvement and means we have more chances of spotting problems or areas of mismatch.

However, we did also give feedback to the cliquey team and listened to their understanding of the problem. As a result, we made a couple of changes to that team – we added people in, took some people away, which gave them a new lease of life. Sometimes teams can stay together for too long.

So you find the right person, then what?

Having put so much time and effort into finding the right person, it is worth thinking carefully about their first days, since this will colour how they feel about their choice to join you. Far too often, people arrive on day one full of excitement and enthusiasm, only to be left to their own devices with no support or friendship offered – sometimes they don't even have a desk to go to! There is a real risk that they will switch off or decide they made the wrong choice and then you are back to square one.

It is worth thinking carefully about their first days.

There are two aspects to the induction process:

▶ introduction to the team
▶ introduction to the business.

Introduction to the team

This is the factor that will have the most impact on whether or not the person bonds with that team. If you have interviewed with the right attitude in mind, even if they don't ultimately fit well in your team, they may be just right for another team in the organisation, so all will not have been lost. However, that will only be possible if they like the workplace and that lies in your hands.

Let us look at some examples of how to do this well.

Ian Martin, at DTC

Ian realised the importance of this when he brought Anni and Benji into his team. He had made real efforts to set up the initial team with strong values and positive working relationships, so wanted that to continue. He arranged for them to be included in a company induction, but also set out to make their first day really welcoming.

As everyone would be impacted by the new arrivals, Ian talked with the team and they worked out a plan together that addressed all the different elements of settling into a new place:

▶ the whole team went for breakfast together outside the office so they could relax and get to know each other better

▶ Mike, an established team member, took Benji and Anni on a tour of the building and the surrounding area, shops, banks etc

▶ Ian talked them through the company values and behaviour that had been agreed with the team

▶ Ian also set up a series of lunches with the people they needed to know from outside the team.

The end result is a positive pair of team players who were quickly integrated into the working style of their particular team.

Helena Moore, at Bromford Housing Group

Helena puts just as much care into integrating her newcomers. She believes in starting the relationship as soon as possible after the person has accepted the role and successful references have been taken up. She:

▶ calls them straight away or sends a congratulations card

▶ invites them to come and meet the team and have a look around before the official start date

▶ makes sure that they are included in the two formal introduction days, when new colleagues get the chance to meet people plus find out more about their particular job and Bromford overall

- invites them to attend team meetings prior to their arrival, if possible, with the aim of building allegiance and commitment from the outset
- sets them up with a buddy on day one, so that they feel fully supported and always have someone to turn to for information.

Then there are the helium balloon and chocolates on their desks! (*See also Chapter 7.*)

The themes of introduction to the team

Again, there are some themes that we can draw from these examples.

- *Give core information* – Decide what people need to know about the job, team and organisation – the values you work to, style of relating, how you celebrate – all the things that make your team special.
- *Involve the team* – Talk with the team members and decide how to welcome newcomers. Do you want to do this in the workplace or would you prefer to meet them on neutral territory? If so, find a time, either before or on arrival, when you can best do that.
- *Make the first day special* – Think about how to make the introduction memorable, but keep it true to how you really are as a team. Don't set up expectations you can't meet.
- *Make sure that they feel supported* – Have people in the team ready to answer questions, show them the ropes, tell them if they behave in a way that is out of line and include them in team activities until they feel able to do so themselves.

Introduction to the work

I bet you remember the first day in your new job and the feeling that you hadn't a clue what to do and any moment you would be found out! It is a pivotal moment for many people and can colour how they feel about the team and their job, so planning how to introduce people to their work will be of real value.

Let's look at some examples of best practice in this area.

Paul Dunmore, at Thomson Directories

Let's track the recruitment of Adam, who proved to be such a star talent for Paul Dunmore.

> For the first couple of weeks I left him to make his own mistakes, but we spoke after each appointment so we could talk through the learning. The first week he sold nothing and got very impatient with himself, so all my energy went into keeping him calm, but his pace and urgency were just right for the job and he soon sold three in one day. In week three, I went out with him to watch, encourage and talk through what worked and didn't work. I also assigned him a buddy so he had someone to call other than the boss – there was nothing he'd go through that this person wouldn't understand, so it ensured help was available all the time. Since our work is all bonus-driven, the buddy gets a bonus when their protégés reach their numbers to ensure they don't lose out.

Tesh Kataria, at Tower Homes

Tesh has a similar approach. He sets out to explain everything as if the person has 'come from Mars and knows nothing', although he is also very careful not to patronise.

Having explained the work, he gives the person a plan of action and leaves them to it, but at the end of each day has an informal discussion to find out how it has all gone and to decide the plan for the next day.

Fran Rodgers, at Northampton Borough Council

Fran Rodgers talks to new arrivals about her preferred management style and how she wants them to work together. She makes it clear that she considers their relationship to be significant and she will give them the support they need, so they must ask if they have a problem.

On day one, she gives them the bare bones of the job, then sends them out to explore before sitting down together to discuss the issues. Her main message is that 'your job is crucial and my job is to help you do it'.

The themes of introduction to the work

So, what ideas can you take away from these examples to try with your new people?

▶ *Let them have a go* – If appropriate for the type of work, let them have a go and discover for themselves what is involved. Make sure that they know you expect them to make mistakes and be available to talk so they learn from the experience.

▶ *Give your time freely* – Sit with them, give feedback, answer questions and provide encouragement. Being generous with your own time at the outset will start the relationship really well.

▶ *Pair them up with a buddy* – Give them someone who knows the business to relate to, so they can ask questions and air concerns. If this will impact on the work of the buddy, make sure that this is acknowledged in some way.

▶ *Be consistent* – Make sure that everything you do is consistent with the team and business culture. Don't set up expectations that mean your new recruits will be disappointed after the first couple of weeks.

Summary

▶ Poor recruitment will cost you, so giving time at the outset is money in the bank.

▶ Developing a strong interview process allows you to understand the people in front of you and helps you see if they will suit the team and the work. Make sure they can also get a good look at the job and the organisation.

▶ Be known for giving quality feedback, both to new arrivals and those who fail to get in.

▶ Make induction a really positive experience, so people feel excited about their new work. Involve the team in the welcome and make it pleasant for everyone.

▶ Make sure that the early days are a good experience with plenty of support to help them get to grips with the job. Provide a buddy for and support them yourself when they need it.

Action plan

If you are about to recruit, take the following action to make sure the outcome is a success.

Today

▶ Check the advert that is going out to the press or circulated internally within the company. Does it describe accurately what and who you want?

▶ If not, talk with whoever is responsible for placing the ad and hold fire until you can make it more accurate and appealing.

Two weeks before the interview

▶ Work out a plan for the interview process. If this isn't your area of expertise, ask for help.

▶ Bring others into the process as a second opinion and factor in some time for the interviewee to experience the actual work.

▶ Look for ways to include the team so they can have an input in the decision-making process.

One month prior to new recruits' arrival

▶ Consider inviting them to a team meeting or including them in any team events.

One week prior to new recruits' arrival

▶ Make sure that you understand the organisation's induction plan and book a place for your recruit as soon as possible. Delay in attendance is a statement of low value.

▶ Think about how you would like to welcome the person into the team and make sure day one is memorable in a positive way.

If you have recently taken on new people

If you feel that the welcome was not all it could be, take steps to amend this.

▶ Arrange a team event to celebrate their being part of the team.

▶ Include other team members in your planning and use their ideas wherever you can.

▶ Ask team members to take responsibility for including the new member and use it as a way to bring the whole team closer together.

▶ Act on this as soon as you can.

CHAPTER

13

Building recognition into your day

'Be positive – it is infectious and gets people enthused, which is very productive.'

John Montgomery, DTC

'Why would you get up every day if you weren't appreciated?' That is Charlotte Butterfield's rationale for keeping up the level of recognition in her team at Badenoch & Clark. The last thing she wants is for her high performers to go elsewhere because they don't feel valued.

It is a fundamental need of human beings to feel appreciated and cherished. Think back to the last time you worked really hard on a project only to have your manager tell you what was wrong with it and nothing at all about what you had done well. My guess is that you felt demoralised. You want to improve, but without some comment about what is good, you lose the will to live!

“ It is a fundamental need of human beings to feel appreciated and cherished. ”

People go to work with an extra spring in their step when they work for an inspirational manager because they feel well cared for and valued. Paul Dunmore, at Thomson Directories, has always believed in creating the right environment for his people, so they feel both physically comfortable and emotionally supported. I visited him just before Christmas when his team members were up against it trying to make appointments with distracted customers. He realised just how hard their job was going to be, so set up fairy lights around the desks, played Christmas music on his iPod and brought mince pies in for coffee time on the last day they were all together before the holiday. They still had to sit on the phone to set up appointments for the week ahead, but at least they felt a bit more Christmassy and knew that he had recognised how much effort they were making.

Find your own limits

I know the idea of fairy lights may provoke an allergic reaction in some people, but don't let that put you off overtly acknowledging the efforts of your team. It is just a matter of working out what they will like and what you can deliver.

It comes back, once again, to knowing your people. As an inspirational manager, your job is all about building relationships, which includes discovering the most appropriate way to recognise your people's amazing successes or valiant mistakes. If you are in any doubt, find an opportunity for a celebration and ask what they would like to do.

« Building relationships ... includes discovering the most appropriate way to recognise your people's amazing successes or valiant mistakes. »

The first thing to consider is your own willingness or lack of it. Before you begin to think about what suits your team, decide what *you* are willing to do. Going totally outside your comfort zone won't come over as real and you will just end up feeling uncomfortable. Of course, if you suspect that you might actually love being a bit more wacky or demonstrative, then go for it. Otherwise, look for your own style.

Action

▶ Revisit your fondest memories of celebrations in your life. What did you do? What were the elements that made it so special for you?

▶ Clarify the situations that make you most uncomfortable. What are the elements that you really can't stand?

▶ Taking the two extremes into account, what is the middle course that you would be able to do wholeheartedly?

Keep these factors in mind as you read the rest of this chapter. It is important to do what you can for your team, but you don't want them distracted by worrying if you are OK.

Do fun and work mix?

For many people, fun is something that remains strictly outside the workplace, but inspirational managers recognise that getting the balance right between 'head down' pressure and having a good time ensures that people feel valued for all their hard work, which inevitably contributes to top-quality results.

Using fun to demonstrate that you appreciate the effort made is a great way to recognise people, but there is a word of warning – you need to understand how *your* people define fun. Failing to do this will only show that you don't care enough to find out what they enjoy and your best intentions will end up setting you back instead of taking you forward.

It is really worth making the effort on this one because people are definitely more productive when they are enjoying themselves – tasks are exhilarating rather than hard work and even boring jobs undertaken with a good bunch of people can be a delight. In contrast, when people don't enjoy their work, time moves really slowly and they have to drag themselves through every step. This is not what an inspirational manager wants to see.

❝ People are definitely more productive when they are enjoying themselves. ❞

If we describe fun as everything from having a laugh to the satisfaction of delivering demanding targets together, then the idea of creating a 'fun' atmosphere at work makes more sense. For example:

▶ in workplaces where people do repetitive work, a light distraction or a bit of laughter will help them keep going

▶ in highly competitive organisations, setting up team and/or individual challenges helps to maintain focus

▶ where specific behaviour is demanded, prizes and awards provide a goal to reach for

▶ in highly technical, expert workplaces, keeping up the challenge with plenty of problems to solve is a delight in its own right.

Recognition isn't just about saying 'thank you'. It is also about acknowledging when work is tough and giving a helping hand. You need your team to be focused and a bit of appropriate fun will help them. For example, if your people droop mid-morning or get tired in that drowsy time after lunch, this might be the exact moment for a little treat. This can range from having a cuppa together, holding a five-minute meeting to share new ideas or successes or, like Tesh Kataria, at Tower Homes, stop them for a quick game to get the energy flowing again.

Equally, if you manage a remote team and its members have to work alone most of the time, bringing them together for work and social time demonstrates that you recognise just how hard this can be. Andrew Rothesay, at Boehringer Ingelheim, has a regular monthly overnight meeting for his team. Sure, they are working most of the time, but the opportunity to have a drink and a good meal together in the evening helps reduce their isolation.

In contrast, at Data Connection, fun is solving a knotty problem and coming up with new and amazing ideas, so the manager needs to make sure that team members have time to bounce their thoughts around. Developing new software requires a truly enquiring mind, so the chance to share and challenge each other's ideas is fantastic and the best way to show just how much you value their contributions.

People need to know they are valued

The COI has found that regular staff events work well for them. Each year they have a fantastic party in the rose garden adjacent to their offices. A public service organisation, there are always concerns about spending too much public money, but they also recognise the need to celebrate and say 'thank you' for all the hard work. That way, people will do good work again next year, serving the public exceptionally well.

They have a whole series of awards:

- ▶ Leader of the year
- ▶ Best campaign
- ▶ Top bloke
- ▶ Top girl

▶ Best performance at a team outing

▶ ABC – Above and Beyond the Call of duty

▶ Ace award, for good ideas.

Oliver Hickson recently won Best performance at a team outing. His award sits in pride of place on the windowsill – a little London bus set on an upturned basket. Nothing snazzy or expensive, but clearly meaningful.

The COI also has a Christmas party for those who want to attend – for example, a boat on the Thames with a subsidised bar. Like many public-sector organisations, the COI competes with the private sector for talent, even though salaries are considerably lower. However, it finds that some high performers are willing to reduce their income for the chance to give something back, which makes it particularly important to show appreciation. In comparison with what their people give up, a subsidised bar and a boat is the least of it!

Getting to grips with validation

There is a simple fact about human behaviour – what gets recognised, gets done. Money is usually the first means of recognition, but is not enough on its own. Paying attention to and showing appreciation for people's inputs demonstrates how important they are to you. We all want approval and attention, so the key is to ensure that recognition reinforces the right attitudes, behaviour and outputs.

But recognition isn't just about the positive things. It also means respecting someone enough to care when they are doing poor work or when they are struggling with relationships. Paying attention and helping them sort these things out is another key way to show how important they are to you and the team.

❝ *Recognition isn't just about the positive things ... It also means respecting someone enough to care when they are doing poor work or ... struggling.* ❞

221

First of all, decide:

- what you need to validate
- what will happen if you don't validate
- who you need to validate
- how to help people through the tough times.

What you need to validate

Think about the impact on you when someone said 'That was great – thank you'. My guess is that it inspired a glow, a feeling that it was worth all the effort and that maybe, just maybe, you would be prepared to do it again. That is one of the main reasons for celebrating success. It encourages people, so they are more likely to make the same or more effort next time you ask.

We are back to our analogy of being a parent. When you need children to behave in a particular way – to do their homework, tidy their rooms, be nice to Granny – you make a fuss when they do it right. The more you demonstrate your delight, the more likely they are to do the same again. As adults we are no different – we respond well to encouragement.

So, you need to identify the key behaviours you are looking for in your team and the outputs that need to be delivered:

- if you lead a customer service team, like Allison Nicoll at Freedom Finance, then you reward calls answered or customer satisfaction
- if the work is about recruiting people for jobs, like Badenoch & Clark, then you reward successful placements
- if you want to build a strong team ethic where people support each other whenever possible, like the team at Tower Homes, then you take the team away for a treat when they deliver exceptional outputs together.

Don't forget the 'thoughtful mistakes and glorious attempts' that Alan Bishop, at COI, referred to. If you want to deliver consistently high-quality work, set new standards of best practice or create new products, mistakes will have to be made. As long as they come from considered attempts to improve or do something more effectively, they will take you forward. So, talk them through, highlight the areas for change or development and congratulate the person for taking the calculated risk.

Action

- Decide on the specific attitudes and behaviours you want to develop or maintain in your team.

- Clarify the impacts they will have on the team's outputs if these behaviours are embedded in day-to-day practice.

- Identify which aspects of the team tasks highlight these attitudes and behaviour and think about how to validate them. Make a list of the tough times, demands or bottlenecks of the last week to guide you to the areas that need attention.

What will happen if you don't validate?

Knowing the answer to this question is at least as important as knowing what to validate. When you fail to recognise people for what they do or don't do, you make a negative impact. So, inspirational managers always provide feedback of some sort, knowing that if they don't people will give up, lose heart or just stop doing their best. Ignore a whole team and they will join forces against the 'common enemy' which is great for building camaraderie, but if that common enemy is you, then it is a disaster!

❝Always provide feedback of some sort.❞

When someone is not delivering quality work, you have to give the tough feedback, but you can make it beneficial by linking it with an offer of support, appreciation of any efforts to change or a plan of action to move them to a better job. If you don't go for one of these options, there may well be a harmful impact on the other members of the team because they:

- agree that the person is not performing, but lose confidence in your ability to manage it effectively

- think that you are being unfair and move in to support the 'underdog', which again means that they unite against you.

The person concerned will feel that there is little point in trying to get it right for you, but, at least if they can get the support of their colleagues, they feel vindicated. However, the result is a split team and no movement towards better performance.

I worked with someone who tried incredibly hard to deliver to very taxing deadlines. It meant working until 8 or 9 p.m. each night of the week for a very long time, which she didn't mind because it was good to feel part of the team and make a contribution to the future of the organisation. But, then the manager asked for a meeting and spent 30 minutes pointing out all the things that had gone wrong. The staff member was gutted and all that willingness went out of the window. She is still with the company, but leaves at 5.30 p.m. each day, regardless of demands. It just doesn't feel worth making the effort any more.

« All that willingness went out of the window. »

Action

▶ Think back over the last week and work out how many times you have been negative about someone's work or attitude.

▶ Look back on their behaviour since that time, especially in relation to yourself, and consider how they responded to your negativity.

▶ Now give some thought to the whole team – have people taken sides on the issue?

▶ Depending on the extent of the reaction, take time with the person to:

  ▶ give them feedback about what they do well

  ▶ clarify the reason for the negative comments and help the person look at how to adapt appropriately.

Who you need to validate

You will have some people in your team who are successfully doing the job they were asked to do and some who are going 'beyond the call of duty'. The inspirational manager realises that both need validating. It is a common view in business that if someone is doing the job they are paid for, there is no reason to compliment them. The truth is that money alone will only get you to 'good enough' work or short-term effort. If you want long-term consistent efficiency, you have to give positive recognition and respect, even when it *is* 'just their job'.

There are lots of ways in which to give that recognition. For example, you can:

- say 'thank you' to them personally or in front of other people, depending on which will mean most to them
- put them forward for a company award
- use your budget to provide a celebration outside work.

The young lady mentioned above didn't need much – just a few words of thanks would have kept her energy focused by confirming her belief that she was adding value. Recognition reinforces the behaviour that you are looking for and its absence implies that the behaviour or attitude being demonstrated is not valued.

Action

- Identify your top performers and the extra efforts that they have made recently. Look for the best way to reinforce this behaviour.
- Think about your good performers and the key milestones that they have achieved recently. Choose the main activities and behaviour you want to reinforce and find the appropriate style for them.
- Identify your average performers and see if there is something they do really well that would give you an opportunity to encourage them.
- Take every chance that comes your way over the next week to say 'thank you' or show your enthusiasm for the good work being done in these situations.
- Make a regular note in your diary to remind you about 'thank you's. If you do nothing else, at least do this on a regular basis.

How to help people through the tough times

Recognition isn't only about celebrating success but also showing people you care even when the going gets tough. They need to see that you recognise that:

- work will be demanding and painful, as often as it will be exciting and special
- mistakes will happen, even when they are trying really hard to deliver their best work
- they won't always behave in the way you need them to.

If they can see that you are on their side, smoothing the way and both supporting and challenging them to do their best work, they will feel encouraged and valued. When they feel like that, the tough times tend to smooth out or at least be times of pulling together in a way that bonds the team further.

❝If they ... feel encouraged and valued ... the tough times tend to smooth out or at least be times of pulling together in a way that bonds the team further.❞

Oliver Hickson, at COI, had a situation where there was friction between two people in the same team. Their manager spoke to her own manager and they agreed to speak to the two of them together to get the problem out in the open. They began by saying, 'This is not acceptable. We are not casting blame, but we don't need this kind of atmosphere in the office, so let's talk about the problem and see what we can do.' Taking the time and effort to let them know where they stood and offer support was enough to bring about better behaviour.

Inspirational managers pay attention to the dynamics of their teams as well as the needs of individuals and, when they see problems, they take action. The end result is that people feel valued and well cared for at all times.

Action

▶ Is anyone in your team having a bad time – at home or at work? If so, show your concern by having a quick chat and see if there is anything you can do to help. If the problem is work-related, make it clear that you want to help by having a one-to-one to discuss it and work out a plan of action.

▶ Think about the relationships within your team and between your team and others. Identify the problems that need to be addressed, plus the significant people involved.

▶ Arrange a meeting to talk to them and find out how you can help them move forward. Make sure that you act on any promises you make – failure to do so will undo all your good work.

▶ If you are part of the problem, ask someone else to come in and help. This may be another manager or an HR representative. Make it clear to the people involved that you really want to resolve the issue so you can all work well together.

How to celebrate success

Begin by finding out what your people like, so that you can design a celebration that suits them. For example, Helena Moore, at Bromford Housing Group, went out to the garden centre to buy a small strip of bedding plants for a keen gardener in her team. The cost was minimal, but the impact huge – it showed that she really cared and wanted to give the best 'thank you' possible.

Be prepared to make an effort

Della Garmory, at Nationwide, makes a big effort to tailor recognition to the individual so it is special and different.

I had a team member who covered for me while I was on holiday and it was a hell of a two weeks. When I came back to work on Monday, she took me through all she had done and it was absolutely brilliant.

During our conversation she happened to say that she liked my shoes. I told her that I'd bought them in a sale over the weekend, so she asked me, 'If you go to that shop again could you get me a pair? I really like them.' So, I made a point of going back to that shop the following weekend and getting a pair in her size. On Monday, I wrapped them up and put them on her desk with a card saying, 'You don't need a new pair of shoes to go that extra mile. Thank you!'

When she opened them, she said 'thank you' and offered me the money. I said 'No, no, no, it's to say thank you for covering for me.' She was amazed, so I pointed out that she had picked up a really tough situation for me, so the least I could do was share my shoes with her!

When you do something meaningful, the real message is not the gift or action but the fact that you went out of your way for them and that makes them feel really special.

If your organisation has a system for celebrations make the most of it for your people and nominate them for annual awards, monthly celebrations or customer service awards whenever you can. Just the fact that you have nominated them will make an impact even if they don't win the award.

If you have a team budget, use it all up and adapt your ideas to suit the person concerned. For example:

- if the person likes razzmatazz, take the team out for a drink at the end of the day and say a public 'thank you'
- produce a small team award – like Oliver Hickson's bus trophy – and put on a mock award ceremony at coffee time
- buy cakes for the team meeting and say a few words about excellent work done, naming the person or not according to their personality
- give the person money to take their partner/friend/child out for a meal at the weekend
- ask your boss to come in to the team for a cuppa and buy a box of chocolates or some flowers to be presented to the person who has gone the extra mile
- buy some theatre vouchers for your resident thespian or tickets for the match for a football fanatic.

Take care that you suit your ideas to the person. Some people will love a bit of fuss, and others will never forgive you, so be sensitive to what they would want.

❝ Take care that you suit your ideas to the person. ❞

The other big trap to avoid is giving what *you* would most like to receive. It is a very common reaction when thinking of doing something nice as we are our own primary benchmark. One Christmas, my husband wanted a special chain lube oil for his bicycle and, once I had worked out what it was, I couldn't think of anything worse. A book, nice clothes or theatre tickets sounded a much better option to me, but past experience had taught that me they would receive a less than enthusiastic response. So, I went round to the bike shop to find exactly the brand he wanted. That £4.50 tube was one of the most appreciated presents I have ever managed to give him. So, keep looking for your team's version of the lube oil!

Action

▶ Work out which members of your team enjoy sharing their success with others and which ones prefer to celebrate quietly out of the limelight.

▶ Keep a small notebook with details of people's hobbies, likes, dislikes, birthdays and interests. Note down ideas as they come to you so that you have a list to refer to when you need to think of something appropriate to show recognition.

▶ Check your ideas with others in the team who know the person really well to make sure it is not just your preference.

Making recognition part of the working day

You will have realised by now that recognition comes in a wide range of forms – from saying a simple 'thank you' to a big event – so there is definitely something you can include in the working day without reducing outputs. In fact, it might even improve results.

There are two types:

▶ work-based recognition

▶ recognition outside work.

Work-based recognition

Use all the means at your disposal to make the most of talented people. Allison Nicoll, at Freedom Finance, had someone in her team who was exceptionally good on the telephone, so she wanted to do all she could to encourage her. Allison herself had been asked to provide some third-party training for one of the company's prime customers, so she invited Danielle to accompany her and support the training process. Not only was this a great way to give her a treat, get her out the office for a while and do something entirely different, but it also began to develop her skills in other areas.

The more you think outside of the normal range of activities the more valuable this process can be, in terms of recognition and for the business.

▶ Make your one-to-one sessions a time that people treasure by giving plenty of acknowledgement as well as looking at problems and development areas. Don't underestimate the power of saying, 'You are not good enough in this area yet, so I am going to do all I can to help you develop.' It is a real sign of your respect and faith in their talent, which means a huge amount to high-potential people. Della Garmory's efforts enabling two people to swap roles (see Chapter 10) is a perfect example of how effective this approach can be.

▶ Saying 'thank you' takes next to no time or effort, so there is no excuse for not doing it. The impact of a manager taking a moment to perch on the desk and say a quick word of thanks is profound. A handwritten note left on the keyboard first thing in the morning is another easy way to do this and it still has a big punch. I have seen people who have kept these cards for years – that's how important they are.

▶ Surround your business plan with celebrations of milestones reached. Ian Martin, at DTC, used part of a team day to identify the main milestones in the project plan and the team members chose what they would do together to mark the occasion. Sometimes it was just the team and sometimes partners were included. The ideas all worked well – except the concert, but at least no one liked it and it makes for a great after-dinner tale!

▶ You can also make business development about celebration and fun. Defining the organisation's vision and future is best done by involving as many people as possible and the process of achieving this can be great fun. Spending a day together thinking about where you are going will mean time together, thinking in a different way, plus a bit of social time.

Know your people

'You need to understand that you can't treat everyone the same.' So says Tesh Kataria, at Tower Homes. Remember, his daily mantra is 'I'm important and I want to be respected.' That means finding out what each person needs, including what they will enjoy by way of celebration. The very act of building relationships is a sign of recognition that means people feel really valued and appreciated.

▶ When a new person joins the team, Tesh goes out to lunch with them on the first day, as a way of getting to know a bit more about them.

▶ The team members follow suit, as demonstrated when Wendy joined – she had lunch with someone every day for the first two weeks, by which time she felt very much part of the team.

▶ Tesh never walks into the office without having a quick word with everyone.

▶ He remembers what is happening in people's lives and asks about how it is all going and takes the time to listen.

The other fabulous way to get to know team members is to work alongside them. Tesh takes advantage of work pressures to do just this. Recently, they decided to gather more customer feedback – a tall order when you plan to call 300 customers direct. Of course, they still had to deal with business as usual, so the task was completed over a number of late nights. Tesh got in the pizzas to bring a party feel to the proceedings and stayed to work with them. Add in a bit of competition, to see who contacted the most people, and you have the makings of a positive evening where the team really enjoyed working together.

I have to tell you – it works. I met the people in Tesh's team and they are an absolute delight. Their ages range from 17 to 50, which could easily bring problems of its own, but they have a wonderful relationship with each other and I have rarely laughed so much in a meeting! They go away together for weekends when targets have been reached and look for any opportunity to celebrate. If you want to see a happy office, this is definitely one to go to!

Recognition outside work

This is about stopping work for a time to say 'thank you' for the extra effort made, so it needs to be planned carefully. Part of the point of it is that you are willing to put the person before the task for a while. To stop work for a cuppa and a cake to celebrate people's birthdays is a real statement of how important they are. Not only that, they will probably work much better and more effectively as a result, in which case it is time well spent.

There are a number of factors you need to take into account.

▶ *The ability of the whole team to take time out to join in* – If you need to have some people in the office during work hours, find a time outside work when they can all be together or break the team into two groups and celebrate twice.

▶ *The location of your workplace* – If you are outside of town, it may not be easy for the team to gather socially after work and people may have a long commute, so consider using lunchtime or talk with them to find a better option.

▶ *The make-up of your team* – If your people have families, they will have childcare arrangements to deal with. You need to organise your celebrations around this or they will feel excluded and resentful.

▶ *The age span and ethnicity of your team* – People may have very different ideas about what constitutes a celebration, so you have to work with them to decide the best ways to mark positive events.

▶ *Work pressures* – When people are under the cosh, make sure that your action really is a support, and not just making life harder.

Involving family and friends

When people have done well, they want to share their excitement with the people who matter to them most. There is nothing better than having your family or friends witness the appreciation of your boss and the team. It is a matter of pride and something that inspirational managers set out to encourage, making the definition of 'family' as wide as possible. Most people have a significant other in their lives somewhere, be it a parent, sibling, partner, child or friend.

Some managers make a point of doing something that includes family at least once a year. As Paul Dunmore, at Thomson Directories, says, 'Family put up with the tough stuff of work all year round – they need to get some of the benefits. In that sense they are an extension of your team.'

❝ Family ... are an extension of your team. ❞

Ask your team members if they would like their work colleagues to meet their 'home' people or whether they prefer the idea of a night out on their own.

A final word

Many teams need to employ temps and contract workers at some time or another. The question always arises, are they part of the team or not? Whether they are or not, they will do their best work if you treat them with respect. You have a real opportunity for a win here as this is something that doesn't often happen to temps.

Tesh makes a point of treating temporary workers in exactly the same way that he treats others and they love him for it. Recognition always works – appreciate what all people do and it will pay off in spades. You will get a better return for your team, too, whether they are with you for one week

---

Summary

▶ Human beings work better when they feel valued and are enjoying themselves.

▶ Get to know what your people enjoy, and if the celebration involves you, make sure it is something you can be wholehearted about.

▶ Validated behaviour will be repeated, so pick out the behaviours and people you want to encourage.

▶ Dealing with problems in a timely manner is a sign of respect, so don't let difficulties fester. ➤

- Match the celebration to the person – be wary of giving what you would like to receive.
- Use work challenges to show your commitment to people and encourage their development.
- Fit celebration into the working day and take into account 'home' needs.
- Include family and friends as appropriate and don't forget temp and contract workers.

Action plan
Today

- Make a note of what matters to each person in your team – family members, hobbies, interests, things they hate. If you don't know, arrange a time to meet them for a natter and find out.
- Give some thought to your own preferred style and see how this links with the team members' personalities.

Next week

- At your team meeting, talk about the targets and milestones that you are presently working towards. Identify the key ones and decide together how you will celebrate achieving them.
- Make a point of saying 'thank you' to at least one person per day.

Next month

- Find an opportunity to work alongside your team and get to know life from their perspective.
- If you don't already have one, ask your manager for a small fund to spend on rewarding your team and be prepared to put forward a business case for it if necessary.
- Look for an opportunity to involve someone in different work – a project or work on site with a customer, for example. Don't restrict yourself to high-flyers, but include those who do a good, steady job every day.

The leader in every manager

'Be your own person, not someone who can be moulded.'

Elliot Whitehead, Boehringer Ingelheim

Getting up every day just to make money will eventually feel pointless and demoralising. People want to add value, to feel that they have contributed to both the business and life around them in a positive way. Providing this context is just one of the leadership tasks that inspirational managers take on wholeheartedly because it matters to them, too.

What is the difference between leading and managing?

First of all, don't think about leading and managing as roles, think about them both as:

- ▶ tasks you take on at different times in your day
- ▶ perspectives you hold in different situations.

Inspirational managers understand that every leader has to manage and every manager has to lead. In fact, they embrace and enjoy the different perspectives, using them both for the good of their people and the organisation.

❝ *Every leader has to manage and every manager has to lead.* ❞

The management task is:

- ▶ To take responsibility for the day-to-day running of the organisation, ensuring that tasks are completed effectively, so that the money keeps coming in and everyone has a job.
- ▶ In addition, managers help their teams and direct reports to do their best work – they support them, develop them to build the talent pipeline of the organisation, keep them focused on the task at hand and deal with problems as they arise.

The leadership task is:

- To pay attention to the big picture and tend the future of the business in the marketplace to make sure that the money keeps coming in, so everyone has a job.
- To watch the market and consider the impact changes will have on the business, develop an inspiring vision and high-level strategy, for the best way forward, and ensure that everyone is bought in and working to the same goals.
- Above all else, to inspire trust, so that people believe the business is in safe hands.

Whatever your official title, as an inspirational manager you know that you have to fulfil both roles. The difference lies in how much time you give each element. If you are a frontline or middle manager, delivering results via your people will take up the bulk of your time, but you still need to help them see how their work fits in to the big picture. As a leader, you must manage your people, do appraisals, deliver tough messages and develop talent, but it will take up less time than your big picture thinking and strategy development work.

There is a tendency to make more of leaders. Forests have been decimated to produce books telling of leadership exploits and quotes have been used prolifically to direct us all to behave in specific ways. Who hasn't heard of Jack Welch and the fabulous tales of Richard Branson? It is all good stuff and we can learn a huge amount from their experience, but inspirational managers such as Oliver Hickson, Fran Rodgers and Ben Wood have just as much to teach us about leadership.

The inspirational manager as leader

As an inspirational manager, your leadership task incorporates:

- building the team's vision for the future

- holding the daily task in the wider contexts
- understanding the strategy business
- building trust
- identifying market opportunities.

Building the team's vision for the future

Inspirational managers are exceptional at supporting their people to deliver strong results. They achieve this, in part, by providing an inspiring vision to work towards. They realise the important role vision has to play in every work situation:

- it builds a picture of what the future will look like, so we have goals to focus on
- once we have this focused picture in our minds, we look for evidence in the external world to confirm it, which reinforces the strength of the picture
- once the picture is strong enough, our minds automatically seek out opportunities that will make it come true.

Think about the last time you wanted to change your car. My guess is that as soon as you started to think seriously about it, you suddenly realised that a load of other people had gone out to buy them, too. Of course, the cars were always there, your mind just wasn't programmed to see them – it took your new interest to bring them into focus. It is the same when you paint an exciting picture of future success – your people will begin to focus on it and see opportunities that they couldn't see before.

Your senior leaders will build this vision for the organisation and it is your task to inspire your team members so that they want to join in. They need to understand where their work fits in and why, and feel really excited and committed to doing it. You will only achieve this when you engage your people at the heart level as well as building a rationale for why it matters, because it is our emotions that drive us to exemplary performance. This is the task of a leader.

❝It is our emotions that drive us to exemplary performance. ❞

Oliver Hickson, at COI, has always believed in articulating a strong vision so that the team know where they are going. 'This means that we can have complete consensus about our direction. So, we have always had away days where we set parameters, develop our business plan and work out people's objectives so everyone is in agreement. After all, we are in this together.'

Action

▶ Think about the organisation's vision and the key ways in which your team contributes to achieving this.

▶ Build a picture of what it will look like, sound like and feel like in the team when everyone is working towards that vision. Your job is to sell this picture to the team, so it must be worth reaching for.

▶ Develop a vision that engages both the 'feeling' *and* the 'thinking' parts of people – an inspiring story plus a clear rationale.

▶ Have a team discussion about the vision. Begin with the organisation's vision, then share your picture in an inspiring way. This is a real opportunity to give up your inhibitions and show your people how excited you are about the possibilities for the team.

▶ Once they have heard your ideas, talk about what it means for them and discuss any ideas and changes that they might suggest. The more involved they are, the more meaningful the vision will become.

▶ Arrange a follow-up meeting to finalise the team's vision and talk through the strategy. Again, make it clear that you really want their ideas and inputs.

Holding the daily task in their wider context

There is nothing more demoralising than doing the same work over and over without understanding why you are doing it. People either turn off, seek out a distraction to liven up the day or find a more meaningful job, because everyone wants to do work that adds value in some way.

There are two ways to make the work more meaningful.

▶ First encourage people to see how they help others in the organisation to be successful. No team works in isolation, although it is easy to get into a rut of just delivering the agreed outputs. Provide a context by demonstrating how dependent other teams are on them doing a good job and they will immediately feel valued and see the work as being worthwhile.

▶ Second, help them to see how their work benefits the end customer or the community. This is all about seeing the value of the work to the outside world and it may require you to think more widely than usual about the purpose of what you all do.

I worked once with an insurance company that had a big call centre population. The managers realised that they could choose to define success as either answering a high volume of calls or giving exceptional customer care. They made the company's vision to 'help people get on with their lives'. From then on, managers reminded people that they were 'helping Mrs Smith get back into her house after a flood', rather than just bringing down the numbers on the 'calls waiting' board. Altogether more satisfying and worthwhile.

Helping your people to see the value they add as they go about their daily work is your leadership task as an inspirational manager, because they want to go home feeling positive and proud about their contribution. For some, this is more straightforward. For example, at Tower Homes, Tesh Kataria and his team get a great buzz every time a nurse or policeman is given the keys to their own home. Equally, Oliver Hickson's team, at COI, can feel positive when they send out an advert directing people to literacy classes. Selling diamonds, creating software and arranging loans are not so obviously 'worthy', but, nonetheless, serve a useful purpose in our society. The more your team members can see why they are doing their daily tasks, the more commitment they will have to delivery.

Action

▶ Think about the impact your team makes and what will happen if they seriously underperform. Which teams will be directly affected and unable to do their own work as a result? What will the impact be on the effectiveness of the business? ➤

> ▶ In your next team meeting, set some time aside for this discussion. Take your people through the same thinking process and get them into a discussion about the impact of their work. They may come up with interlinkages you hadn't thought of.
>
> ▶ Get a big piece of paper and draw a map of the interrelationships between your team and others and how this impacts on the business. Put it up in the office and refer to it at regular intervals, pointing out how their good work is making it easier for the next team in the chain.
>
> ▶ Think about why you all do the work. Find your equivalent of 'helping people get on with their lives'.
>
> It is the old adage: a tiler can see herself laying bathroom tiles or creating a beautiful home. One is a lot more exciting than the other and seeing it in that context makes the task feel a lot more worthwhile.

Understanding the strategy business

Thinking as a leader requires you to understand the business as a whole. Getting everyone excited about the vision is a fantastic start, but you can't stop there – at least not if you want to remain a credible inspirational manager. You need to develop a strategy for the team that will contribute to the success of the organisation's vision.

A strategy is the high-level plan of action for how the vision will be achieved. Inspirational managers take the organisation's strategy and break it down for their teams. This enables them to:

▶ understand the direction of the team and the contribution they make

▶ break down the task into manageable chunks and create a timeline for their completion

▶ identify links with other parts of the business and external customers

▶ make the vision real.

Not only is this helpful for the success of the task, it addresses the familiar problem of the silo mentality. When people see how their work connects with and enables others, they are less likely to empire build, which makes for much better service all round – internal and external.

Understanding the business strategy helped Ben Wood to realise that he needed to include both the external contractor and the client as part of Mace's project team. He could see that the overall success of the business would suffer if they didn't all cooperate. He could have stayed in his team bubble and let the failures happen without taking any responsibility, but that would just have prolonged the work, cost the client dear and stopped the business being so successful.

As inspirational managers work on team strategy, they pay attention to how their team impacts on other parts of the business. They collaborate with manager colleagues to maximise the team's effectiveness, which is not only good for the business, but gives people a real sense of being part of a bigger entity and experience of how other teams work. This linking people together to deliver a big picture strategy is the work of a leader and one that sits well with the desire of inspirational managers to maximise talent and deliver strong results.

“Linking people together to deliver a big picture strategy is the work of a leader.”

Action

▶ Look at your team's vision and strategy alongside the business's vision and strategy. Draw out a plan or mindmap of the linkages between teams and business areas. Identify situations where your work depends on other people delivering effectively and where others depend on your team.

▶ Write down the requirements for each situation and make a second list of how effective/supportive the delivery has been to date. If there are gaps to be addressed, include this in the team's strategy.

▶ Map out the key deliverables and time frames involved and mark the interlinkages. Give each deliverable a rating in terms of its importance to the overall success of the business.

▶ Once you have had a first pass at drawing up this strategy, take it to your team and get your people's input. Listen to their ideas and discuss concerns, then agree how to move forward together.

▶ Keep the vision and strategy in the forefront of their minds so it can do its job of inspiring them to action.

Leading the team in a turnaround

Fran Rodgers took on her job as Corporate Manager for Housing Services at Northampton Borough Council when it was really struggling. Joining a team with such a major turnaround task meant that she couldn't work in isolation. Of course, not everyone has such extreme issues to deal with, but the lesson of keeping your head up to see what is going on around you is well worth heeding.

Part of the problem she faced was the silo nature of the organisation, where people had little connection to the big picture, even though they were doing such useful work.

Fran and her team deal with all issues relating to housing – homelessness, tenancy management, temporary accommodation and housing advice. There is little more fundamental to our well-being than the roof over our heads, so these teams are highly significant to the people of Northampton.

For Fran, the main reason for working is to make a difference, so an important part of her inspirational manager style is to underline and clarify 'the way we serve'. However, she came into a team who were cut off from the value of their work, functioning badly as a result and experiencing little job satisfaction. So, her first task was one of leadership, helping her people to understand where their work fitted into the big scheme of things and begin to develop a sense of pride in their day-to-day achievements.

The team members weren't used to working in her naturally collaborative manner, so Fran needed to make tough decisions and give very clear instructions.

> Fundamentally, I'm an enabler, but I do have very high standards, so I wasn't going to settle for second best. I had to use the iron fist in a velvet glove. I did it nicely, but they were left in no doubt. I became more dictatorial temporarily. I found that, unless I was exceedingly clear, people didn't believe that I meant it, so just didn't do what they were asked.

When a business is in such a difficult position, you can't just manage your way out of it – you *have* to employ leadership skills. Fran had to get the good people thinking in a different way and the only way to do this was to inspire them with a vision of life in the future. They needed to crave it with all their hearts and be determined to make the necessary changes, regardless of the demands that placed on them.

Building trust

Both leaders and managers need to build and maintain trust. As an inspirational manager, you create a trusting environment within which your people can do their best work. The leadership aspect is to demonstrate that you care not just about your own team but are invested in the success of the whole organisation. In this way, you will extend your influence and ensure that you are listened to by other people in your organisation.

Never underestimate the impact that this will have on your team. The familiarity that comes from working together day after day encourages them to take for granted the care and concern you show them. For them to recognise that managers and leaders throughout the organisation listen carefully to what you say and are inspired by your approach to the business will bring new respect and energy. They will see you through the eyes of other people and feel proud – a great fillip to any team.

❝ They will see you through the eyes of other people and feel proud. ❞

Fran Rodgers realised that she had to build strong relationships in both her team and across the organisation to ensure she could use her experience and understanding for the good of customers:

▶ She could see the changes that needed to be made, so set about making those that were in her sphere of influence.

▶ To influence on a wider scale, she called on the trusting relationships she had built across the organisation. By working closely with colleagues from different areas, she could put forward ideas and ensure that her knowledge and understanding were not confined to just one part of the service.

It will be just the same for you. As you widen your view of the organisation and put the work of your team into context, you will see things that work exceedingly well and could be shared more widely. You will also see things that don't work and your slightly 'external' eye will bring a clarity that is not available to those involved. If you don't have trusting relationships, you will be unable to act and the organisation will lose out.

Action

▶ Take a good look at your work relationships outside of your team, decide which are the most important and give them marks out of ten for the level of trust – 10 for a high level of trust to 1 if it is non-existent. How are you doing with those in closest proximity to you?

▶ Highlight the names that are most significant to the work of your team. If you rated those relationsips below six, decide what you have to do to improve trust.

▶ If you have a poor track record with any of the significant people, give some real thought to how you can create change. As an inspirational manager, you can't afford to hold grudges. *Everyone* makes mistakes and you have to move on.

▶ Put dates in your diary and meet with someone outside the team each week for a coffee and catch up. Ask for feedback on your team's outputs and your own and pick their brains as to how you might improve.

▶ Make sure that you include senior people in your list. You may need to get ideas and information up the hierarchy, so build at least one link to the level above you, in addition to your own manager.

Identifying market opportunities

Inspirational managers build good networks outside as well as inside their organisations. If you want the business to thrive, you need to know how your competitors are faring. The ease with which you can achieve this depends on your sector. In retail, you just have to go shopping to see how they are doing and your team members can do the same. In other sectors, you will need to use your contacts or go to conferences and general meetings whenever you can.

Your network can also help you keep abreast of market forces. Understanding the impacts of terrorism, variable weather patterns and the latest celebrity's dress sense can determine whether you are ahead or behind the game. Don't leave it all to senior managers, although they should be as keen as you to ensure that the company is leading edge.

As you sit within your business or service, you will have specific ideas that can help improve outputs. Some managers have great ideas but hold on to them because they don't see it as their place to suggest changes. However, doing that means you are falling down on your job. Your senior leaders aren't perfect, so they need your insight. It is a bit like in the field of medicine – when a GP needs help, they involve a specialist. You are the specialist in your area of work, so share your knowledge and understanding freely with your senior leaders.

> **Share your knowledge and understanding freely with your senior leaders.**

Action

▶ Read the business press and trade journals regularly. If you don't normally have time for a newspaper, take one on a Sunday and hold on to the business section for your week time reading. Alternatively, arrange for Web alerts in your specific business area.

▶ Encourage your team members to do the same so that they can grow their market knowledge, which will also increase their commitment to the organisation.

▶ Find out about relevant conferences and go to at least one a year.

▶ Set up a lunch for managers across the business and suggest having a monthly meeting to talk about the sector and what is changing.

▶ Find a way to check how your competitors are doing. Explore what they do differently, look for ideas you can pinch and consider how to improve your competitive advantage.

This is one of those additional tasks that inspirational managers do so well, increasing their value to the business and their teams. You don't have to do it all at once – one step at a time will be fine. You will be amazed at how quickly these behaviours become second nature.

The main thing to remember is that you are not just managing your team, you are contributing to the whole organisation. You have specialist knowledge to add to the smooth and successful running of the service or business. As you progress up the hierarchy, the balance between leadership and management will change, but, wherever you are in the business, you will always have to manage *and* lead.

Summary

▶ Leaders and managers do both jobs – it is just the proportions that vary.

▶ The leadership role for a manager begins with building a vision for the team that reflects its contribution to the company's vision.

▶ The team members need to understand how their work fits into the business context, so that they can make sense of what they contribute to the success of the organisation.

▶ Building a team strategy will keep the team aligned and demonstrate the value of joint working with other teams.

▶ Without trust, none of this will be possible. High levels of trust call for open and honest relationships.

▶ Keeping an eye on your competitors is an important part of remaining at the leading edge of your sector, so take every opportunity you can to stay in touch.

Action plan

Today

▶ Look at your networks and give them marks out of ten, as suggested above. Decide where you need to focus your attention.

▶ Set time aside in your diary to begin work on your vision and strategy. Keep it in the back of your mind as you run up to the allocated time, so you already have ideas when you begin.

Next week

▶ Talk with the team members and alert them to the concept of vision and strategy to start them thinking. Agree a time when you will share your vision with them – this will help you stick to doing it, not that easy in a busy management job!

▶ Mention one way in which the team has helped the business to move forward in your team meeting, being clear about how your people have contributed to the success.

▶ Read the business news at least once in the week, whether in a newspaper or on the Web. Find out one thing about your competitors and look at the implications for your organisation.

➤

Next month

▶ Arrange a longer team meeting and talk through your vision and strategy. Allow plenty of time for ideas and comments. If you have a garrulous team, then allow at least two hours. If your people are more reticent, keep it short, but build discussion into meetings on a regular basis so that they get more used to it. Make it clear that their comments are really helpful.

▶ Consider inviting other people to come to your team meeting to talk about their work and join in discussions.

▶ Bring some of your colleagues together to talk generally about the business. Explain to them why you are doing this and see if you can excite someone else about developing their leadership skills.

▶ Make sure you include a colleague you trust and ask them for feedback on your ability to inspire. Do the same after your team meeting – ask someone you believe will tell you the truth and get some feedback on how you presented the vision.

▶ If you struggle with the idea of being inspiring, ask for help. HR will help you sort out some presentation skills training or arrange some time with an inspirational speaker in your business.

Appendix 1: Who are these inspirational managers?

Charlotte Butterfield
Badenoch & Clark
www.badenochandclark.com

Charlotte joined Badenoch & Clark in 1997, having worked as a private detective for a year after graduating from the University of East Anglia. Charlotte initially worked on the locum team, recruiting lawyers for all sectors before specialising in private practice.

She was promoted to manager of the private practice locum team in 2000 and then went on to manage four more teams in 2003 – namely, the legal finance temporary team, legal finance permanent team, legal secretarial temporary team and legal secretarial permanent team. Charlotte was promoted to senior manager in September 2005 and won Badenoch & Clark's Manager of the Year award in October 2005.

Charlotte focuses on new business, account development and training and developing her team members. She has 7 direct reports and overall responsibility for 15 people. She has worked on national accounts such as Freshfields Bruckhaus Deringer and Herbert Smith.

Paul Dunmore
Thomson Directories
www.thomsondirectories.com

At the time of writing, Paul was Senior Line Manager in Field Sales. He was responsible for coaching 7 salespeople whose responsibilities were to achieve revenue and productivity targets in 11 of the Thomson Local Directories in Yorkshire. His revenue target was in excess of £1.6m.

Since then, Paul has been promoted to Office Sales Manager for Yorkshire and the North East. He is now responsible for 5 field sales managers, 33 sales people and 6 support staff. His revenue targets are in excess of £8.0m and he is responsible for 23 directories.

Della Garmory
Nationwide Building Society
www.nationwide.co.uk

Della has worked at Nationwide Building Society for 17 years and, during this time, held several roles within the HR Division.

She has recently been promoted to Head of HR Business Partners, within the new infrastructure for Nationwide's HR Division. She is responsible for a team of HR business partners, who provide a full HR consultancy service to a diverse range of clients at several sites throughout the country.

She thoroughly enjoys working for Nationwide and the people agenda is at the front of the organisation's strategy.

Many of her management practices are taken from the sporting arena. As a keen sportswoman, she believes that everyone has the potential to succeed in whatever they do there.

Oliver Hickson
Central Office of Information (COI)
www.coi.gov.uk

Oliver left St Andrews University in 1990 to join Guinness PLC as a management trainee in sales/marketing. Three years later, after extensive marketing training, he joined Alan Pascoe Associates, a sports marketing agency in account management and new business.

In 1995, Oliver joined the COI as a sponsorship manager in a team of four with a turnover of £200,000.

Oliver has progressed through the ranks and is now Director of PR & Sponsorship with a team of 35 and a turnover of over £25m. The area is now comprised of four business disciplines, which are sponsorship (broadcast, events, partnership marketing), PR (national and regional), merchandising and black and minority ethnic marketing.

Tesh Kataria

Tower Homes
www.towerhomes.org.uk

Tesh joined Tower Homes on Valentine's Day 2000 and it's been a love affair ever since!

Tower Homes specialises in providing affordable housing for people on low to moderate incomes who are unable to afford London house prices. In 2006, Tower Homes was voted Sunday Times Best Small Company to work for.

As Sales Manager, Tesh manages a team of 11 staff who help customers to buy or rent an affordable home via a government-funded housing scheme. Between 2004 and 2006, his team helped 1223 key workers in London to get on the property ladder. The target was 961.

Following a promotion in September 2006, Tesh now also manages the Central Communications Team at Tower Homes, which consists of a further 13 staff, working on the frontline of Tower's customer interface.

Tesh also enjoys a strategic role, regularly meeting with government bodies and key stakeholders.

Nic Larkin
Data Connection
www.dataconnection.com

Data Connection is a UK company that develops communications software. Most of the big players in the computer industry are customers of one or more of its products.

Nic's division is working on a software product called a session border controller – the key ingredient that will enable the Internet to support reliable phone services. He and his team of three design, write and maintain parts of the computer code from which the product is built. Their work is abstract and technical, so first line managers like him need to be very hands-on, with small team sizes to maintain a tight focus.

Most of his time is spent discussing specific tasks and issues with his team or doing technical work himself. He is a true techie at heart, so being able to carry out a share of the development work personally keeps him sane and remains a very satisfying part of the job.

Ian Martin
Diamond Trading Company
www.dtc.com

Ian's role as Pricing Manager for the Diamond Trading Company (the marketing arm of De Beers) is to set prices for all of De Beers' diamonds that are purchased and sold worldwide – a total of $6b per annum. Over the past two years, his team has had to review the company's pricing methodologies.

Inspired by the vision of the young and dynamic managing director, Ian has been able to draw on his experience of over 25 years with the De Beers family of companies, which has included living and working in Australia, Belgium, Botswana, India, South Africa, plus numerous visits to the Far East. The knowledge that he gained in these previous roles has helped him to support the modernisation process of a rather traditional company. This change in the business ethic provided a platform for him to have greater freedom of expression within his working environment.

Seeing his team develop has been extremely fulfilling for him and his own learning has been that giving either positive or constructive feedback is a very rewarding experience.

Helena Moore
Bromford Housing Group
www.bromford.co.uk

Helena has spent all her housing career with Bromford. This has given her the opportunity to be involved in the rapid growth, change and development of the group's people, products and customer experience delivery.

Helena started as a 'frontline' housing officer, moving through a number of roles and secondment opportunities to became head of the group's largest housing region. Then, in 2005, she became Group Director of Communications and Business Excellence.

Her three favourite responsibilities are developing her own team, developing the group's 'Delivering great customer experience' strategy and involvement in the 'Great place to work' team. This has involved compulsive stealing of good practice and innovation to ensure strategic continuous improvement and to support frontline colleagues to deliver a great service to customers.

Her favourite motto, which she pinched from a friend, is 'Get a job you enjoy and never work another day in your life!'

Allison Nicoll

Freedom Finance

www.moneyexpert.com

Alison has worked at Freedom Finance for the last five and a half years as a contact centre manager, handling the operations of both inbound and outbound loans and mortgages at the Wilmslow site of 90 employees. She has been heavily involved in numerous projects, including the implementation of the dialler into a different site.

Alison has recently moved to Alliance and Leicester, within the Commercial Bank sector. Her role is to oversee Resource Planning, System Development and Performance Quality.

Fran Rodgers

Northampton Borough Council

www.northampton.gov.uk

Fran works for Northampton Borough Council as Corporate Manager for Housing, Revenues & Benefits. She is responsible for 5 service managers and 166 staff and also manages an external partnership arrangement. She has worked in local government for 23 years but been in her present post since September 2005. She has been tasked with delivering rapid improvements in a poor performing authority and to work corporately with her colleagues on a range of cross-functional services.

She enjoys a challenge and gets great job satisfaction from helping others to develop their skills and abilities. It is particularly motivating for her to be involved in improving services to the council's customers.

Andrew Rothesay

Boehringer Ingelheim (BI)
www.boehringer-ingelheim.co.uk

Andrew is from Edinburgh, 40 years old and married. He has a BSc and an MBA and has worked for BI UK for nearly eight years in a variety of sales and marketing positions. He has recently moved to BI's corporate office in Germany.

Boehringer Ingelheim is a research-driven group of companies dedicated to researching, developing, manufacturing and marketing pharmaceuticals that improve health and quality of life. Its vision is 'Value through innovation'.

Boehringer Ingelheim has almost 36,000 employees in 144 affiliated companies spread around the globe, with approximately 1000 employees in the UK. Its headquarters is in Ingelheim, the German town where the company was founded in 1885. The company remains family owned.

Ben Wood

Mace
www.mace.co.uk

Ben's role within Mace was to lead the business and first-class lounges project at the new Heathrow Terminal 5.

Mace was appointed as both project and construction manager, to manage and lead a team of professional consultants – architects, engineers, quantity surveyors and interior designers – to design and achieve sign-off from the British Airways stakeholders. Mace then procured the works packages and managed the 20 contractors required to build the lounges.

Ben had 15 Mace employees working for him. His main role was to quickly generate team spirit and give direction – to the different companies and

Mace employees alike – while also maintaining the commercial tension that would give the client best value.

During August 2006, Ben was given the fantastic opportunity to take over a family firm, so he regrettably resigned before the BA project was completed. In November 2006, Ben took up his new role, which he is finding equally challenging and rewarding.

Appendix 2: Inspiration

Inspiration comes in many forms and different things affect different people. It's not important what inspires you, just that you let it!

What follows are some thoughts from different sources:

▶ short quotes from some of the inspirational managers in the book, talking about the things that have inspired them

▶ some contacts that might be of value as you progress in your journey towards becoming an inspirational manager

▶ a few books that might be useful further reading for you.

Inspirational managers share their sources of inspiration

I asked some of the managers featured in the book to tell us what has influenced their approach to people.

Nic Larkin, Data Connection

I find those TV programmes where Gordon Ramsay goes in and tries to rescue failing restaurants interesting from a people management perspective. At one moment he gives direct feedback in an incredibly effective way and the next moment he is rude, counterproductive and puts up people's defences. Trying to understand what distinguishes the two can be quite enlightening.

Of course, Ricky Gervais in *The Office* needs careful study by all managers!

Fran Rodgers, Northampton Borough Council

If pushed, I would choose Bill Shankly as the representative of my love for football. I chose him because of his passion for the game, ability to create successful teams, vision and leadership.

He always knew how important the game was to ordinary people, hence the quote, 'Football is not a matter of life and death, it's more important than that!'

I could go on!

Oliver Hickson, COI

Personal coaching has been really inspirational for me.

I play a lot of tennis, so I often reference to myself the good and less good coaching I have received!

Also, *Henry V* by Shakespeare – when Henry managed to stir up his troops before Agincourt.

Paul Dunmore, Thomson Directories

The experiences I've had with bad managers have inspired me to do my own research work and find out what makes an inspirational manager. From my findings, I learned many things. Quotes that stay with me include:

▶ 'Most of what we call management consists of making it difficult for people to get their jobs done.'

Peter Drucker

▶ *'Relationships with people* inspire them to follow. A leader makes *other people* feel important.'

Unknown

▶ Involve your people:

'No one is ever 100 per cent supportive of a direction they had no part in formulating.'

'People need their ideas incorporated or understand why they are not.'

Unknown

A great source of inspiration was *'It's Much More Important Than That': Bill Shankly: The autobiography* by Stephen F. Kelly (Virgin, 1997).

Being from Liverpool, I was brought up in the period of the late, great manager, Bill Shankly. He inherited an average team and then went about convincing his players that they were, in fact, the greatest. His inspirational leadership gave them a confidence above and beyond anything they had previously had and then the results followed. He even went to the lengths of changing the colour of their shorts, kitting them out in an all-red strip (previously they had white shorts), making them feel bigger and stronger.

Andrew Rothesay, Boehringer Ingelheim

What has influenced my approach to people?

▶ The values instilled by family and friends.

▶ My experiences of managers and leaders, both good and bad.

▶ Early read books dealing with people's motivations such as *Animal Farm* by George Orwell, *Macbeth* and *Hamlet* by Shakespeare.

More latterly, the management writings of Peter Drucker, Charles Handy and Tom Peters.

Finally, 'For a' that', a poem by Robert Burns.

Charlotte Butterfield, Badenoch & Clark

Charlotte actively looks for inspiration and finds it in all sorts of places. She loves listening to what members of her team have to tell her and this often provides ideas for how to move forward.

She is also a great reader, devouring a book a week, most of which offers up something in the way of inspiration. *The Alchemist: A fable about following your dream* by Paulo Coelho (HarperCollins, 1999) is one that she has found useful.

Having recently returned from a holiday in Australia, she was struck by the frequent use of the word 'vitality' and is now determined to build this into the team and its vision for the future.

Tesh Kataria, Tower Homes

The book that has greatly influenced both my management style and my personal life is *How to Win Friends and Influence People* by Dale Carnegie (Vermilion, 2007). The title says it all and, as far I'm concerned, it's the 'bible of human interaction' and should be taught in all schools!

More recently, I have taken inspiration from the Jamie Oliver documentary *Fifteen*. Watching Jamie transform delinquent teenagers into top chefs taught me how having faith in others, even when they have lost faith in themselves, can achieve amazing results.

Useful addresses

Great Companies Consulting (GCC)

Contact: Judith Leary-Joyce at judith@greatcompaniesconsulting.com *Tel*: 01727 765521

Provides help with the development of Inspirational Managers and Employer of Choice culture.

360-degree feedback

For further information on the 360-degree feedback, outlined in Chapter 2, contact Great Companies Consulting (details given above).

Academy of Executive Coaching

Contact Sue Simmons at: sue@academyofexecutivecoaching.com *Tel*: 01727 864806

Provides courses for managers wanting to develop their coaching skills.

The Greenleaf Centre for Servant-Leadership UK

Contact: John Noble at www.greenleaf.org.uk/conferences.html *Tel*: 020 8715 2205

Holds a regular conference and workshops on subjects of interest to inspirational managers. To find out more about its programme, visit the website given above.

Books to read

If this book has whetted your appetite, you may want to read around the subject some more.

If you want to explore the process part of the management, try:

▶ *Brilliant Manager: What the best managers know, do and say* by Nick Peeling (Prentice Hall, 2006).

▶ *The Manager's Book of Checklists: Everything you need to know, when you need to know it* by Derek Rowntree (Prentice Hall, 2005).

The Chartered Institute of Personnel and Development (CIPD) has a wide range of books on all kinds of management issues. You can take a look at its selection by visiting its website at www.cipd.co.uk/Bookstore

To extend your understanding of coaching, the following book is a good read:

▶ *Coaching to Solutions: A manager's toolkit for performance delivery* by Carole Pemberton (Butterworth-Heineman, 2006).

Action learning has been mentioned a number of times in the book. If you want to find out more, you might start with:

▶ *Action Learning: A practical guide* by Krystyna Weinstein (Gower, 1998).

For some useful basics on business behaviour, set out in an easy-to-follow way, try:

▶ *The Rules of Work: A definitive guide to personal success* by Richard Templar (Prentice Hall, 2002).

Take time to read each rule carefully and decide what you think and feel about it. Sometimes the first impression is rather odd, but mostly they are appropriate to the approach of inspirational managers.

I can highly recommend the following book on management, which has been a real inspiration to me:

▶ *Love and Profit: The art of caring leadership* by James A. Autry (Avon, 1992).

You may also find his new book interesting since it deals with how to handle tough situations, which is the hallmark of an inspirational manager:

▶ *The Book of Hard Choices: How to make the right decisions at work and keep your self-respect* by James Autry (Morgan Road, 2006).

The section on personal vision in the following book is useful and would be good background reading for your development as an inspirational manager:

▶ *The Seven Habits of Highly Effective People: Powerful lessons in personal change* by Stephen Covey (Simon & Schuster, 2004).

Index

and openness 106
setting charter 103–4, 121
strong framework 102–11
and strong relationships 105, 121
team's communication to you 110–11
via business goals 107–8
via personal learning 108–9
your communication to team 110
teams
 inspirational 31, 101–2
 manager's distance from 119–20
 problem 115–16, 121–2
 taking your place 61
 and truthfulness 29
 values 18
 virtual 131
terminating employment 190–4, 195
 content of interview 193–4
 decisiveness 191
 legalities 192–3
 planning the process 193
 truthfulness 193–4
Thomson Directories 20, 45, 251–2
 see also Dunmore, Paul
360–degree feedback 11–12, 72, 76,
  262
 questionnaire 11, 12–13
tough conversations 181–96
 see also performance conversations
tough love 18
tough times
 recognising 225–6
 and support 125
 and truthfulness 29–30
Tower Homes 34–5, 64–5, 81, 101, 253
 talent-spotting 164–5
 validation 222
 see also Kataria, Tesh
trust 5, 29, 30, 101

appraisal meetings 135
building 245–6, 248
and senior level 246
truthfulness 27, 35, 61
 and delegation 152–3, 158
 terminating employment 193–4
 tough conversations 186–7, 195
 and trust levels 29–30, 36
 and underperformers 19

underperformance 183, 188–9
 and appraisals 127
 dealing with 19
 reasons for 181
understanding others 44–6, 52
 action plan 45–6
understanding yourself 43–4, 52
upward management 32–5
 extreme 71–3

Valentine, Hazel 80
validation 221–6
 behaviour needing 224–5
 encouraging behaviour 221, 222–3, 233
 impact of lack of 223–4
 see also recognition
values, organisational 32–4, 36
valuing people see recognition
virtual teams 131
vision, building 238, 239–42
 and deliverables 242–3

Whitehead, Elliot 237
Wood, Ben 5, 32, 48, 125, 243, 257–8
workload
 assessment of team's 149–50
 and delegation 149–50, 159
 reducing 142–3
workplace design 117–19, 121